-4425

MW01051799

THIS IS YOUR **PASSBOOK**® FOR ...

AIRPORT POLICE/ARFF OFFICER

NLC®

NATIONAL LEARNING CORPORATION®
passbooks.com

PASSBOOK® SERIES

THE *PASSBOOK® SERIES* has been created to prepare applicants and candidates for the ultimate academic battlefield – the examination room.

At some time in our lives, each and every one of us may be required to take an examination – for validation, matriculation, admission, qualification, registration, certification, or licensure.

Based on the assumption that every applicant or candidate has met the basic formal educational standards, has taken the required number of courses, and read the necessary texts, the *PASSBOOK® SERIES* furnishes the one special preparation which may assure passing with confidence, instead of failing with insecurity. Examination questions – together with answers – are furnished as the basic vehicle for study so that the mysteries of the examination and its compounding difficulties may be eliminated or diminished by a sure method.

This book is meant to help you pass your examination provided that you qualify and are serious in your objective.

The entire field is reviewed through the huge store of content information which is succinctly presented through a provocative and challenging approach – the question-and-answer method.

A climate of success is established by furnishing the correct answers at the end of each test.

You soon learn to recognize types of questions, forms of questions, and patterns of questioning. You may even begin to anticipate expected outcomes.

You perceive that many questions are repeated or adapted so that you can gain acute insights, which may enable you to score many sure points.

You learn how to confront new questions, or types of questions, and to attack them confidently and work out the correct answers.

You note objectives and emphases, and recognize pitfalls and dangers, so that you may make positive educational adjustments.

Moreover, you are kept fully informed in relation to new concepts, methods, practices, and directions in the field.

You discover that you arre actually taking the examination all the time: you are preparing for the examination by "taking" an examination, not by reading extraneous and/or supererogatory textbooks.

In short, this PASSBOOK®, used directedly, should be an important factor in helping you to pass your test.

AIRPORT POLICE OFFICER

DUTIES

An Airport Police Officer is a sworn peace officer, authorized to carry a firearm who enforces federal and state regulations, city ordinances, and security, traffic, fire and safety rules and regulations; engages in law enforcement activities, including uniformed foot, vehicle, motorcycle, bicycle patrol and plainclothes assignments; makes arrests; writes reports; provides information to the public regarding locations and operations of the Department; and does related work.

HOW TO TAKE A TEST

I. YOU MUST PASS AN EXAMINATION

A. WHAT EVERY CANDIDATE SHOULD KNOW

Examination applicants often ask us for help in preparing for the written test. What can I study in advance? What kinds of questions will be asked? How will the test be given? How will the papers be graded?

As an applicant for a civil service examination, you may be wondering about some of these things. Our purpose here is to suggest effective methods of advance study and to describe civil service examinations.

Your chances for success on this examination can be increased if you know how to prepare. Those "pre-examination jitters" can be reduced if you know what to expect. You can even experience an adventure in good citizenship if you know why civil service exams are given.

B. WHY ARE CIVIL SERVICE EXAMINATIONS GIVEN?

Civil service examinations are important to you in two ways. As a citizen, you want public jobs filled by employees who know how to do their work. As a job seeker, you want a fair chance to compete for that job on an equal footing with other candidates. The best-known means of accomplishing this two-fold goal is the competitive examination.

Exams are widely publicized throughout the nation. They may be administered for jobs in federal, state, city, municipal, town or village governments or agencies.

Any citizen may apply, with some limitations, such as the age or residence of applicants. Your experience and education may be reviewed to see whether you meet the requirements for the particular examination. When these requirements exist, they are reasonable and applied consistently to all applicants. Thus, a competitive examination may cause you some uneasiness now, but it is your privilege and safeguard.

C. HOW ARE CIVIL SERVICE EXAMS DEVELOPED?

Examinations are carefully written by trained technicians who are specialists in the field known as "psychological measurement," in consultation with recognized authorities in the field of work that the test will cover. These experts recommend the subject matter areas or skills to be tested; only those knowledges or skills important to your success on the job are included. The most reliable books and source materials available are used as references. Together, the experts and technicians judge the difficulty level of the questions.

Test technicians know how to phrase questions so that the problem is clearly stated. Their ethics do not permit "trick" or "catch" questions. Questions may have been tried out on sample groups, or subjected to statistical analysis, to determine their usefulness.

Written tests are often used in combination with performance tests, ratings of training and experience, and oral interviews. All of these measures combine to form the best-known means of finding the right person for the right job.

II. HOW TO PASS THE WRITTEN TEST

A. NATURE OF THE EXAMINATION

To prepare intelligently for civil service examinations, you should know how they differ from school examinations you have taken. In school you were assigned certain definite pages to read or subjects to cover. The examination questions were quite detailed and usually emphasized memory. Civil service exams, on the other hand, try to discover your present ability to perform the duties of a position, plus your potentiality to learn these duties. In other words, a civil service exam attempts to predict how successful you will be. Questions cover such a broad area that they cannot be as minute and detailed as school exam questions.

In the public service similar kinds of work, or positions, are grouped together in one "class." This process is known as *position-classification*. All the positions in a class are paid according to the salary range for that class. One class title covers all of these positions, and they are all tested by the same examination.

B. FOUR BASIC STEPS

1) Study the announcement

How, then, can you know what subjects to study? Our best answer is: "Learn as much as possible about the class of positions for which you've applied." The exam will test the knowledge, skills and abilities needed to do the work.

Your most valuable source of information about the position you want is the official exam announcement. This announcement lists the training and experience qualifications. Check these standards and apply only if you come reasonably close to meeting them.

The brief description of the position in the examination announcement offers some clues to the subjects which will be tested. Think about the job itself. Review the duties in your mind. Can you perform them, or are there some in which you are rusty? Fill in the blank spots in your preparation.

Many jurisdictions preview the written test in the exam announcement by including a section called "Knowledge and Abilities Required," "Scope of the Examination," or some similar heading. Here you will find out specifically what fields will be tested.

2) Review your own background

Once you learn in general what the position is all about, and what you need to know to do the work, ask yourself which subjects you already know fairly well and which need improvement. You may wonder whether to concentrate on improving your strong areas or on building some background in your fields of weakness. When the announcement has specified "some knowledge" or "considerable knowledge," or has used adjectives like "beginning principles of…" or "advanced … methods," you can get a clue as to the number and difficulty of questions to be asked in any given field. More questions, and hence broader coverage, would be included for those subjects which are more important in the work. Now weigh your strengths and weaknesses against the job requirements and prepare accordingly.

3) Determine the level of the position

Another way to tell how intensively you should prepare is to understand the level of the job for which you are applying. Is it the entering level? In other words, is this the position in which beginners in a field of work are hired? Or is it an intermediate or advanced level? Sometimes this is indicated by such words as "Junior" or "Senior" in the class title. Other jurisdictions use Roman numerals to designate the level – Clerk I, Clerk II, for example. The word "Supervisor" sometimes appears in the title. If the level is not indicated by the title, check the description of duties. Will you be working under very close supervision, or will you have responsibility for independent decisions in this work?

4) Choose appropriate study materials

Now that you know the subjects to be examined and the relative amount of each subject to be covered, you can choose suitable study materials. For beginning level jobs, or even advanced ones, if you have a pronounced weakness in some aspect of your training, read a modern, standard textbook in that field. Be sure it is up to date and has general coverage. Such books are normally available at your library, and the librarian will be glad to help you locate one. For entry-level positions, questions of appropriate difficulty are chosen – neither highly advanced questions, nor those too simple. Such questions require careful thought but not advanced training.

If the position for which you are applying is technical or advanced, you will read more advanced, specialized material. If you are already familiar with the basic principles of your field, elementary textbooks would waste your time. Concentrate on advanced textbooks and technical periodicals. Think through the concepts and review difficult problems in your field.

These are all general sources. You can get more ideas on your own initiative, following these leads. For example, training manuals and publications of the government agency which employs workers in your field can be useful, particularly for technical and professional positions. A letter or visit to the government department involved may result in more specific study suggestions, and certainly will provide you with a more definite idea of the exact nature of the position you are seeking.

III. KINDS OF TESTS

Tests are used for purposes other than measuring knowledge and ability to perform specified duties. For some positions, it is equally important to test ability to make adjustments to new situations or to profit from training. In others, basic mental abilities not dependent on information are essential. Questions which test these things may not appear as pertinent to the duties of the position as those which test for knowledge and information. Yet they are often highly important parts of a fair examination. For very general questions, it is almost impossible to help you direct your study efforts. What we can do is to point out some of the more common of these general abilities needed in public service positions and describe some typical questions.

1) General information

Broad, general information has been found useful for predicting job success in some kinds of work. This is tested in a variety of ways, from vocabulary lists to questions about current events. Basic background in some field of work, such as sociology or economics, may be sampled in a group of questions. Often these are principles which have become familiar to most persons through exposure rather than through formal training. It is difficult to advise you how to study for these questions; being alert to the world around you is our best suggestion.

2) Verbal ability

An example of an ability needed in many positions is verbal or language ability. Verbal ability is, in brief, the ability to use and understand words. Vocabulary and grammar tests are typical measures of this ability. Reading comprehension or paragraph interpretation questions are common in many kinds of civil service tests. You are given a paragraph of written material and asked to find its central meaning.

3) Numerical ability

Number skills can be tested by the familiar arithmetic problem, by checking paired lists of numbers to see which are alike and which are different, or by interpreting charts and graphs. In the latter test, a graph may be printed in the test booklet which you are asked to use as the basis for answering questions.

4) Observation

A popular test for law-enforcement positions is the observation test. A picture is shown to you for several minutes, then taken away. Questions about the picture test your ability to observe both details and larger elements.

5) Following directions

In many positions in the public service, the employee must be able to carry out written instructions dependably and accurately. You may be given a chart with several columns, each column listing a variety of information. The questions require you to carry out directions involving the information given in the chart.

6) Skills and aptitudes

Performance tests effectively measure some manual skills and aptitudes. When the skill is one in which you are trained, such as typing or shorthand, you can practice. These tests are often very much like those given in business school or high school courses. For many of the other skills and aptitudes, however, no short-time preparation can be made. Skills and abilities natural to you or that you have developed throughout your lifetime are being tested.

Many of the general questions just described provide all the data needed to answer the questions and ask you to use your reasoning ability to find the answers. Your best preparation for these tests, as well as for tests of facts and ideas, is to be at your physical and mental best. You, no doubt, have your own methods of getting into an exam-taking mood and keeping "in shape." The next section lists some ideas on this subject.

IV. KINDS OF QUESTIONS

Only rarely is the "essay" question, which you answer in narrative form, used in civil service tests. Civil service tests are usually of the short-answer type. Full instructions for answering these questions will be given to you at the examination. But in case this is your first experience with short-answer questions and separate answer sheets, here is what you need to know:

1) Multiple-choice Questions

Most popular of the short-answer questions is the "multiple choice" or "best answer" question. It can be used, for example, to test for factual knowledge, ability to solve problems or judgment in meeting situations found at work.

A multiple-choice question is normally one of three types—

- It can begin with an incomplete statement followed by several possible endings. You are to find the one ending which *best* completes the statement, although some of the others may not be entirely wrong.
- It can also be a complete statement in the form of a question which is answered by choosing one of the statements listed.
- It can be in the form of a problem – again you select the best answer.

Here is an example of a multiple-choice question with a discussion which should give you some clues as to the method for choosing the right answer:

When an employee has a complaint about his assignment, the action which will *best* help him overcome his difficulty is to
   A. discuss his difficulty with his coworkers
   B. take the problem to the head of the organization
   C. take the problem to the person who gave him the assignment
   D. say nothing to anyone about his complaint

In answering this question, you should study each of the choices to find which is best. Consider choice "A" – Certainly an employee may discuss his complaint with fellow employees, but no change or improvement can result, and the complaint remains unresolved. Choice "B" is a poor choice since the head of the organization probably does not know what assignment you have been given, and taking your problem to him is known as "going over the head" of the supervisor. The supervisor, or person who made the assignment, is the person who can clarify it or correct any injustice. Choice "C" is, therefore, correct. To say nothing, as in choice "D," is unwise. Supervisors have and interest in knowing the problems employees are facing, and the employee is seeking a solution to his problem.

2) True/False Questions

The "true/false" or "right/wrong" form of question is sometimes used. Here a complete statement is given. Your job is to decide whether the statement is right or wrong.

SAMPLE: A roaming cell-phone call to a nearby city costs less than a non-roaming call to a distant city.

This statement is wrong, or false, since roaming calls are more expensive.
This is not a complete list of all possible question forms, although most of the others are variations of these common types. You will always get complete directions for

answering questions. Be sure you understand *how* to mark your answers – ask questions until you do.

V. RECORDING YOUR ANSWERS

Computer terminals are used more and more today for many different kinds of exams.

For an examination with very few applicants, you may be told to record your answers in the test booklet itself. Separate answer sheets are much more common. If this separate answer sheet is to be scored by machine – and this is often the case – it is highly important that you mark your answers correctly in order to get credit.

An electronic scoring machine is often used in civil service offices because of the speed with which papers can be scored. Machine-scored answer sheets must be marked with a pencil, which will be given to you. This pencil has a high graphite content which responds to the electronic scoring machine. As a matter of fact, stray dots may register as answers, so do not let your pencil rest on the answer sheet while you are pondering the correct answer. Also, if your pencil lead breaks or is otherwise defective, ask for another.

Since the answer sheet will be dropped in a slot in the scoring machine, be careful not to bend the corners or get the paper crumpled.

The answer sheet normally has five vertical columns of numbers, with 30 numbers to a column. These numbers correspond to the question numbers in your test booklet. After each number, going across the page are four or five pairs of dotted lines. These short dotted lines have small letters or numbers above them. The first two pairs may also have a "T" or "F" above the letters. This indicates that the first two pairs only are to be used if the questions are of the true-false type. If the questions are multiple choice, disregard the "T" and "F" and pay attention only to the small letters or numbers.

Answer your questions in the manner of the sample that follows:

32. The largest city in the United States is
    A. Washington, D.C.
    B. New York City
    C. Chicago
    D. Detroit
    E. San Francisco

1) Choose the answer you think is best. (New York City is the largest, so "B" is correct.)
2) Find the row of dotted lines numbered the same as the question you are answering. (Find row number 32)
3) Find the pair of dotted lines corresponding to the answer. (Find the pair of lines under the mark "B.")
4) Make a solid black mark between the dotted lines.

VI. BEFORE THE TEST

Common sense will help you find procedures to follow to get ready for an examination. Too many of us, however, overlook these sensible measures. Indeed, nervousness and fatigue have been found to be the most serious reasons why applicants fail to do their best on civil service tests. Here is a list of reminders:

- Begin your preparation early – Don't wait until the last minute to go scurrying around for books and materials or to find out what the position is all about.
- Prepare continuously – An hour a night for a week is better than an all-night cram session. This has been definitely established. What is more, a night a week for a month will return better dividends than crowding your study into a shorter period of time.
- Locate the place of the exam – You have been sent a notice telling you when and where to report for the examination. If the location is in a different town or otherwise unfamiliar to you, it would be well to inquire the best route and learn something about the building.
- Relax the night before the test – Allow your mind to rest. Do not study at all that night. Plan some mild recreation or diversion; then go to bed early and get a good night's sleep.
- Get up early enough to make a leisurely trip to the place for the test – This way unforeseen events, traffic snarls, unfamiliar buildings, etc. will not upset you.
- Dress comfortably – A written test is not a fashion show. You will be known by number and not by name, so wear something comfortable.
- Leave excess paraphernalia at home – Shopping bags and odd bundles will get in your way. You need bring only the items mentioned in the official notice you received; usually everything you need is provided. Do not bring reference books to the exam. They will only confuse those last minutes and be taken away from you when in the test room.
- Arrive somewhat ahead of time – If because of transportation schedules you must get there very early, bring a newspaper or magazine to take your mind off yourself while waiting.
- Locate the examination room – When you have found the proper room, you will be directed to the seat or part of the room where you will sit. Sometimes you are given a sheet of instructions to read while you are waiting. Do not fill out any forms until you are told to do so; just read them and be prepared.
- Relax and prepare to listen to the instructions
- If you have any physical problem that may keep you from doing your best, be sure to tell the test administrator. If you are sick or in poor health, you really cannot do your best on the exam. You can come back and take the test some other time.

VII. AT THE TEST

The day of the test is here and you have the test booklet in your hand. The temptation to get going is very strong. Caution! There is more to success than knowing the right answers. You must know how to identify your papers and understand variations in the type of short-answer question used in this particular examination. Follow these suggestions for maximum results from your efforts:

1) Cooperate with the monitor

The test administrator has a duty to create a situation in which you can be as much at ease as possible. He will give instructions, tell you when to begin, check to see that you are marking your answer sheet correctly, and so on. He is not there to guard you, although he will see that your competitors do not take unfair advantage. He wants to help you do your best.

2) Listen to all instructions

Don't jump the gun! Wait until you understand all directions. In most civil service tests you get more time than you need to answer the questions. So don't be in a hurry. Read each word of instructions until you clearly understand the meaning. Study the examples, listen to all announcements and follow directions. Ask questions if you do not understand what to do.

3) Identify your papers

Civil service exams are usually identified by number only. You will be assigned a number; you must not put your name on your test papers. Be sure to copy your number correctly. Since more than one exam may be given, copy your exact examination title.

4) Plan your time

Unless you are told that a test is a "speed" or "rate of work" test, speed itself is usually not important. Time enough to answer all the questions will be provided, but this does not mean that you have all day. An overall time limit has been set. Divide the total time (in minutes) by the number of questions to determine the approximate time you have for each question.

5) Do not linger over difficult questions

If you come across a difficult question, mark it with a paper clip (useful to have along) and come back to it when you have been through the booklet. One caution if you do this – be sure to skip a number on your answer sheet as well. Check often to be sure that you have not lost your place and that you are marking in the row numbered the same as the question you are answering.

6) Read the questions

Be sure you know what the question asks! Many capable people are unsuccessful because they failed to *read* the questions correctly.

7) Answer all questions

Unless you have been instructed that a penalty will be deducted for incorrect answers, it is better to guess than to omit a question.

8) Speed tests

It is often better NOT to guess on speed tests. It has been found that on timed tests people are tempted to spend the last few seconds before time is called in marking answers at random – without even reading them – in the hope of picking up a few extra points. To discourage this practice, the instructions may warn you that your score will be "corrected" for guessing. That is, a penalty will be applied. The incorrect answers will be deducted from the correct ones, or some other penalty formula will be used.

9) Review your answers

If you finish before time is called, go back to the questions you guessed or omitted to give them further thought. Review other answers if you have time.

10) Return your test materials

If you are ready to leave before others have finished or time is called, take ALL your materials to the monitor and leave quietly. Never take any test material with you. The monitor can discover whose papers are not complete, and taking a test booklet may be grounds for disqualification.

VIII. EXAMINATION TECHNIQUES

1) Read the general instructions carefully. These are usually printed on the first page of the exam booklet. As a rule, these instructions refer to the timing of the examination; the fact that you should not start work until the signal and must stop work at a signal, etc. If there are any *special* instructions, such as a choice of questions to be answered, make sure that you note this instruction carefully.

2) When you are ready to start work on the examination, that is as soon as the signal has been given, read the instructions to each question booklet, underline any key words or phrases, such as *least, best, outline, describe* and the like. In this way you will tend to answer as requested rather than discover on reviewing your paper that you *listed without describing*, that you selected the *worst* choice rather than the *best* choice, etc.

3) If the examination is of the objective or multiple-choice type – that is, each question will also give a series of possible answers: A, B, C or D, and you are called upon to select the best answer and write the letter next to that answer on your answer paper – it is advisable to start answering each question in turn. There may be anywhere from 50 to 100 such questions in the three or four hours allotted and you can see how much time would be taken if you read through all the questions before beginning to answer any. Furthermore, if you come across a question or group of questions which you know would be difficult to answer, it would undoubtedly affect your handling of all the other questions.

4) If the examination is of the essay type and contains but a few questions, it is a moot point as to whether you should read all the questions before starting to answer any one. Of course, if you are given a choice – say five out of seven and the like – then it is essential to read all the questions so you can eliminate the two that are most difficult. If, however, you are asked to answer all the questions, there may be danger in trying to answer the easiest one first because you may find that you will spend too much time on it. The best technique is to answer the first question, then proceed to the second, etc.

5) Time your answers. Before the exam begins, write down the time it started, then add the time allowed for the examination and write down the time it must be completed, then divide the time available somewhat as follows:

- If 3-1/2 hours are allowed, that would be 210 minutes. If you have 80 objective-type questions, that would be an average of 2-1/2 minutes per question. Allow yourself no more than 2 minutes per question, or a total of 160 minutes, which will permit about 50 minutes to review.
- If for the time allotment of 210 minutes there are 7 essay questions to answer, that would average about 30 minutes a question. Give yourself only 25 minutes per question so that you have about 35 minutes to review.

6) The most important instruction is to *read each question* and make sure you know what is wanted. The second most important instruction is to *time yourself properly* so that you answer every question. The third most important instruction is to *answer every question.* Guess if you have to but include something for each question. Remember that you will receive no credit for a blank and will probably receive some credit if you write something in answer to an essay question. If you guess a letter – say "B" for a multiple-choice question – you may have guessed right. If you leave a blank as an answer to a multiple-choice question, the examiners may respect your feelings but it will not add a point to your score. Some exams may penalize you for wrong answers, so in such cases *only*, you may not want to guess unless you have some basis for your answer.

7) Suggestions
   a. Objective-type questions
      1. Examine the question booklet for proper sequence of pages and questions
      2. Read all instructions carefully
      3. Skip any question which seems too difficult; return to it after all other questions have been answered
      4. Apportion your time properly; do not spend too much time on any single question or group of questions
      5. Note and underline key words – *all, most, fewest, least, best, worst, same, opposite,* etc.
      6. Pay particular attention to negatives
      7. Note unusual option, e.g., unduly long, short, complex, different or similar in content to the body of the question
      8. Observe the use of "hedging" words – *probably, may, most likely,* etc.
      9. Make sure that your answer is put next to the same number as the question
      10. Do not second-guess unless you have good reason to believe the second answer is definitely more correct
      11. Cross out original answer if you decide another answer is more accurate; do not erase until you are ready to hand your paper in
      12. Answer all questions; guess unless instructed otherwise
      13. Leave time for review

   b. Essay questions
      1. Read each question carefully
      2. Determine exactly what is wanted. Underline key words or phrases.
      3. Decide on outline or paragraph answer

4. Include many different points and elements unless asked to develop any one or two points or elements
5. Show impartiality by giving pros and cons unless directed to select one side only
6. Make and write down any assumptions you find necessary to answer the questions
7. Watch your English, grammar, punctuation and choice of words
8. Time your answers; don't crowd material

8) Answering the essay question

Most essay questions can be answered by framing the specific response around several key words or ideas. Here are a few such key words or ideas:

M's: manpower, materials, methods, money, management
P's: purpose, program, policy, plan, procedure, practice, problems, pitfalls, personnel, public relations
   a. Six basic steps in handling problems:
      1. Preliminary plan and background development
      2. Collect information, data and facts
      3. Analyze and interpret information, data and facts
      4. Analyze and develop solutions as well as make recommendations
      5. Prepare report and sell recommendations
      6. Install recommendations and follow up effectiveness

   b. Pitfalls to avoid
      1. *Taking things for granted* – A statement of the situation does not necessarily imply that each of the elements is necessarily true; for example, a complaint may be invalid and biased so that all that can be taken for granted is that a complaint has been registered
      2. *Considering only one side of a situation* – Wherever possible, indicate several alternatives and then point out the reasons you selected the best one
      3. *Failing to indicate follow up* – Whenever your answer indicates action on your part, make certain that you will take proper follow-up action to see how successful your recommendations, procedures or actions turn out to be
      4. *Taking too long in answering any single question* – Remember to time your answers properly

IX. AFTER THE TEST

Scoring procedures differ in detail among civil service jurisdictions although the general principles are the same. Whether the papers are hand-scored or graded by machine we have described, they are nearly always graded by number. That is, the person who marks the paper knows only the number – never the name – of the applicant. Not until all the papers have been graded will they be matched with names. If other tests, such as training and experience or oral interview ratings have been given, scores will be combined. Different parts of the examination usually have different weights. For example, the written test might count 60 percent of the final grade, and a rating of training and experience 40 percent. In many jurisdictions, veterans will have a certain number of points added to their grades.

After the final grade has been determined, the names are placed in grade order and an eligible list is established. There are various methods for resolving ties between those who get the same final grade – probably the most common is to place first the name of the person whose application was received first. Job offers are made from the eligible list in the order the names appear on it. You will be notified of your grade and your rank as soon as all these computations have been made. This will be done as rapidly as possible.

People who are found to meet the requirements in the announcement are called "eligibles." Their names are put on a list of eligible candidates. An eligible's chances of getting a job depend on how high he stands on this list and how fast agencies are filling jobs from the list.

When a job is to be filled from a list of eligibles, the agency asks for the names of people on the list of eligibles for that job. When the civil service commission receives this request, it sends to the agency the names of the three people highest on this list. Or, if the job to be filled has specialized requirements, the office sends the agency the names of the top three persons who meet these requirements from the general list.

The appointing officer makes a choice from among the three people whose names were sent to him. If the selected person accepts the appointment, the names of the others are put back on the list to be considered for future openings.

That is the rule in hiring from all kinds of eligible lists, whether they are for typist, carpenter, chemist, or something else. For every vacancy, the appointing officer has his choice of any one of the top three eligibles on the list. This explains why the person whose name is on top of the list sometimes does not get an appointment when some of the persons lower on the list do. If the appointing officer chooses the second or third eligible, the No. 1 eligible does not get a job at once, but stays on the list until he is appointed or the list is terminated.

X. HOW TO PASS THE INTERVIEW TEST

The examination for which you applied requires an oral interview test. You have already taken the written test and you are now being called for the interview test – the final part of the formal examination.

You may think that it is not possible to prepare for an interview test and that there are no procedures to follow during an interview. Our purpose is to point out some things you can do in advance that will help you and some good rules to follow and pitfalls to avoid while you are being interviewed.

What is an interview supposed to test?
The written examination is designed to test the technical knowledge and competence of the candidate; the oral is designed to evaluate intangible qualities, not readily measured otherwise, and to establish a list showing the relative fitness of each candidate – as measured against his competitors – for the position sought. Scoring is not on the basis of "right" and "wrong," but on a sliding scale of values ranging from "not passable" to "outstanding." As a matter of fact, it is possible to achieve a relatively low score without a single "incorrect" answer because of evident weakness in the qualities being measured.

Occasionally, an examination may consist entirely of an oral test – either an individual or a group oral. In such cases, information is sought concerning the technical knowledges and abilities of the candidate, since there has been no written examination for this purpose. More commonly, however, an oral test is used to supplement a written examination.

Who conducts interviews?

The composition of oral boards varies among different jurisdictions. In nearly all, a representative of the personnel department serves as chairman. One of the members of the board may be a representative of the department in which the candidate would work. In some cases, "outside experts" are used, and, frequently, a businessman or some other representative of the general public is asked to serve. Labor and management or other special groups may be represented. The aim is to secure the services of experts in the appropriate field.

However the board is composed, it is a good idea (and not at all improper or unethical) to ascertain in advance of the interview who the members are and what groups they represent. When you are introduced to them, you will have some idea of their backgrounds and interests, and at least you will not stutter and stammer over their names.

What should be done before the interview?

While knowledge about the board members is useful and takes some of the surprise element out of the interview, there is other preparation which is more substantive. It *is* possible to prepare for an oral interview – in several ways:

1) Keep a copy of your application and review it carefully before the interview

This may be the only document before the oral board, and the starting point of the interview. Know what education and experience you have listed there, and the sequence and dates of all of it. Sometimes the board will ask you to review the highlights of your experience for them; you should not have to hem and haw doing it.

2) Study the class specification and the examination announcement

Usually, the oral board has one or both of these to guide them. The qualities, characteristics or knowledges required by the position sought are stated in these documents. They offer valuable clues as to the nature of the oral interview. For example, if the job involves supervisory responsibilities, the announcement will usually indicate that knowledge of modern supervisory methods and the qualifications of the candidate as a supervisor will be tested. If so, you can expect such questions, frequently in the form of a hypothetical situation which you are expected to solve. NEVER go into an oral without knowledge of the duties and responsibilities of the job you seek.

3) Think through each qualification required

Try to visualize the kind of questions you would ask if you were a board member. How well could you answer them? Try especially to appraise your own knowledge and background in each area, *measured against the job sought*, and identify any areas in which you are weak. Be critical and realistic – do not flatter yourself.

4) Do some general reading in areas in which you feel you may be weak

For example, if the job involves supervision and your past experience has NOT, some general reading in supervisory methods and practices, particularly in the field of human relations, might be useful. Do NOT study agency procedures or detailed manuals. The oral board will be testing your understanding and capacity, not your memory.

5) Get a good night's sleep and watch your general health and mental attitude

You will want a clear head at the interview. Take care of a cold or any other minor ailment, and of course, no hangovers.

What should be done on the day of the interview?

Now comes the day of the interview itself. Give yourself plenty of time to get there. Plan to arrive somewhat ahead of the scheduled time, particularly if your appointment is in the fore part of the day. If a previous candidate fails to appear, the board might be ready for you a bit early. By early afternoon an oral board is almost invariably behind schedule if there are many candidates, and you may have to wait. Take along a book or magazine to read, or your application to review, but leave any extraneous material in the waiting room when you go in for your interview. In any event, relax and compose yourself.

The matter of dress is important. The board is forming impressions about you – from your experience, your manners, your attitude, and your appearance. Give your personal appearance careful attention. Dress your best, but not your flashiest. Choose conservative, appropriate clothing, and be sure it is immaculate. This is a business interview, and your appearance should indicate that you regard it as such. Besides, being well groomed and properly dressed will help boost your confidence.

Sooner or later, someone will call your name and escort you into the interview room. *This is it.* From here on you are on your own. It is too late for any more preparation. But remember, you asked for this opportunity to prove your fitness, and you are here because your request was granted.

What happens when you go in?

The usual sequence of events will be as follows: The clerk (who is often the board stenographer) will introduce you to the chairman of the oral board, who will introduce you to the other members of the board. Acknowledge the introductions before you sit down. Do not be surprised if you find a microphone facing you or a stenotypist sitting by. Oral interviews are usually recorded in the event of an appeal or other review.

Usually the chairman of the board will open the interview by reviewing the highlights of your education and work experience from your application – primarily for the benefit of the other members of the board, as well as to get the material into the record. Do not interrupt or comment unless there is an error or significant misinterpretation; if that is the case, do not hesitate. But do not quibble about insignificant matters. Also, he will usually ask you some question about your education, experience or your present job – partly to get you to start talking and to establish the interviewing "rapport." He may start the actual questioning, or turn it over to one of the other members. Frequently, each member undertakes the questioning on a particular area, one in which he is perhaps most competent, so you can expect each member to participate in the examination. Because time is limited, you may also expect some rather abrupt switches in the direction the questioning takes, so do not be upset by it. Normally, a board member will not pursue a single line of questioning unless he discovers a particular strength or weakness.

After each member has participated, the chairman will usually ask whether any member has any further questions, then will ask you if you have anything you wish to add. Unless you are expecting this question, it may floor you. Worse, it may start you off on an extended, extemporaneous speech. The board is not usually seeking more information. The question is principally to offer you a last opportunity to present further qualifications or to indicate that you have nothing to add. So, if you feel that a significant qualification or characteristic has been overlooked, it is proper to point it out in a sentence or so. Do not compliment the board on the thoroughness of their examination – they have been sketchy, and you know it. If you wish, merely say, "No thank you, I have nothing further to add." This is a point where you can "talk yourself out" of a good impression or fail to present an important bit of information. Remember, *you close the interview yourself.*

The chairman will then say, "That is all, Mr. _____, thank you." Do not be startled; the interview is over, and quicker than you think. Thank him, gather your belongings and take your leave. Save your sigh of relief for the other side of the door.

How to put your best foot forward

Throughout this entire process, you may feel that the board individually and collectively is trying to pierce your defenses, seek out your hidden weaknesses and embarrass and confuse you. Actually, this is not true. They are obliged to make an appraisal of your qualifications for the job you are seeking, and they want to see you in your best light. Remember, they must interview all candidates and a non-cooperative candidate may become a failure in spite of their best efforts to bring out his qualifications. Here are 15 suggestions that will help you:

1) Be natural – Keep your attitude confident, not cocky

If you are not confident that you can do the job, do not expect the board to be. Do not apologize for your weaknesses, try to bring out your strong points. The board is interested in a positive, not negative, presentation. Cockiness will antagonize any board member and make him wonder if you are covering up a weakness by a false show of strength.

2) Get comfortable, but don't lounge or sprawl

Sit erectly but not stiffly. A careless posture may lead the board to conclude that you are careless in other things, or at least that you are not impressed by the importance of the occasion. Either conclusion is natural, even if incorrect. Do not fuss with your clothing, a pencil or an ashtray. Your hands may occasionally be useful to emphasize a point; do not let them become a point of distraction.

3) Do not wisecrack or make small talk

This is a serious situation, and your attitude should show that you consider it as such. Further, the time of the board is limited – they do not want to waste it, and neither should you.

4) Do not exaggerate your experience or abilities

In the first place, from information in the application or other interviews and sources, the board may know more about you than you think. Secondly, you probably will not get away with it. An experienced board is rather adept at spotting such a situation, so do not take the chance.

5) If you know a board member, do not make a point of it, yet do not hide it

Certainly you are not fooling him, and probably not the other members of the board. Do not try to take advantage of your acquaintanceship – it will probably do you little good.

6) Do not dominate the interview

Let the board do that. They will give you the clues – do not assume that you have to do all the talking. Realize that the board has a number of questions to ask you, and do not try to take up all the interview time by showing off your extensive knowledge of the answer to the first one.

7) Be attentive

You only have 20 minutes or so, and you should keep your attention at its sharpest throughout. When a member is addressing a problem or question to you, give him your undivided attention. Address your reply principally to him, but do not exclude the other board members.

8) Do not interrupt

A board member may be stating a problem for you to analyze. He will ask you a question when the time comes. Let him state the problem, and wait for the question.

9) Make sure you understand the question

Do not try to answer until you are sure what the question is. If it is not clear, restate it in your own words or ask the board member to clarify it for you. However, do not haggle about minor elements.

10) Reply promptly but not hastily

A common entry on oral board rating sheets is "candidate responded readily," or "candidate hesitated in replies." Respond as promptly and quickly as you can, but do not jump to a hasty, ill-considered answer.

11) Do not be peremptory in your answers

A brief answer is proper – but do not fire your answer back. That is a losing game from your point of view. The board member can probably ask questions much faster than you can answer them.

12) Do not try to create the answer you think the board member wants

He is interested in what kind of mind you have and how it works – not in playing games. Furthermore, he can usually spot this practice and will actually grade you down on it.

13) Do not switch sides in your reply merely to agree with a board member

Frequently, a member will take a contrary position merely to draw you out and to see if you are willing and able to defend your point of view. Do not start a debate, yet do not surrender a good position. If a position is worth taking, it is worth defending.

14) Do not be afraid to admit an error in judgment if you are shown to be wrong

The board knows that you are forced to reply without any opportunity for careful consideration. Your answer may be demonstrably wrong. If so, admit it and get on with the interview.

15) Do not dwell at length on your present job

The opening question may relate to your present assignment. Answer the question but do not go into an extended discussion. You are being examined for a *new* job, not your present one. As a matter of fact, try to phrase ALL your answers in terms of the job for which you are being examined.

Basis of Rating

Probably you will forget most of these "do's" and "don'ts" when you walk into the oral interview room. Even remembering them all will not ensure you a passing grade. Perhaps you did not have the qualifications in the first place. But remembering them will help you to put your best foot forward, without treading on the toes of the board members.

Rumor and popular opinion to the contrary notwithstanding, an oral board wants you to make the best appearance possible. They know you are under pressure – but they also want to see how you respond to it as a guide to what your reaction would be under the pressures of the job you seek. They will be influenced by the degree of poise you display, the personal traits you show and the manner in which you respond.

ABOUT THIS BOOK

This book contains tests divided into Examination Sections. Go through each test, answering every question in the margin. At the end of each test look at the answer key and check your answers. On the ones you got wrong, look at the right answer choice and learn. Do not fill in the answers first. Do not memorize the questions and answers, but understand the answer and principles involved. On your test, the questions will likely be different from the samples. Questions are changed and new ones added. If you understand these past questions you should have success with any changes that arise. Tests may consist of several types of questions. We have additional books on each subject should more study be advisable or necessary for you. Finally, the more you study, the better prepared you will be. This book is intended to be the last thing you study before you walk into the examination room. Prior study of relevant texts is also recommended. NLC publishes some of these in our Fundamental Series. Knowledge and good sense are important factors in passing your exam. Good luck also helps. So now study this Passbook, absorb the material contained within and take that knowledge into the examination. Then do your best to pass that exam.

———

EXAMINATION SECTION

EXAMINATION SECTION
TEST 1

DIRECTIONS: Each question or incomplete statement is followed by several suggested
answers or completions. Select the one that BEST answers the question or
completes the statement. *PRINT THE LETTER OF THE CORRECT ANSWER
IN THE SPACE AT THE RIGHT.*

1. A law enforcement officer may make an arrest without a warrant when the crime   1.____

    A.   is committed in his presence
    B.   violates airport security
    C.   takes place in a sterile area
    D.   takes place in an exclusive area
    E.   all of the above

2. A private security force must have _____ in order to perform the law enforcement func-   2.____
tion.

    A.   arrest power
    B.   a warrant
    C.   written agreement between the employer and the airport operator
    D.   local approval
    E.   firearms

3. Alternate security procedures to be used during emergencies are to be included in the   3.____
security program when

    A.   ordinary procedures are insufficient
    B.   the airport operator has developed alternate procedures
    C.   alternate procedures include the use of locally deputized law enforcement officers
    D.   the FAA requires the airport operator to go to unreasonable extremes to meet all
        possible security threats
    E.   at all times

4. Disclosure of the airport security program may be prohibited if it   4.____

    A.   contains sensitive information
    B.   will be of value to those who would commit offenses against civil aviation
    C.   would be detrimental to the safety of persons traveling in air transportation
    D.   involves national security
    E.   is not in conflict with the Freedom of Information Act

5. The portion of an airport designed and used for landing, take-offs, or surface maneuver-   5.____
ing of airplanes, is called the _____ area.

    A.   general aviation   B.   air operations   C.   exclusive
    D.   sterile   E.   ground

6. Airport security programs provide for the safety of persons and property against   6.____

    A.   threats of violence
    B.   violations of civil liberties
    C.   any and all damages connected with air transportation

    D. acts of criminal violence and aircraft piracy
    E. hijacking

7. The air carrier should notify the _____ when the procedures, facilities and equipment it uses over an exclusive area are inadequate.   7.__

    A. Regional Director
    B. Law Enforcement Officer
    C. Airport Operator
    D. Civil Aviation Security Inspector
    E. Administrator

8. Each airport operator shall maintain at LEAST one complete copy of its approved security program at   8.__

    A. the Department of Justice
    B. the entrance to each sterile area
    C. the officer of any Civil Aviation Security Inspector
    D. the office of the Regional Director
    E. its principal operations office

9. _____ days are allowed for the approval of a security program?   9.__

    A. 15   B. 30   C. 45   D. 60   E. 90

10. Proposed amendments to the security program must   10.__

    A. be distributed to the air carrier tenants
    B. receive the oral approval of the air carrier tenants
    C. receive written approval of the air carrier tenants
    D. be coordinated with the air carrier tenants
    E. not have any involvement with the air carrier tenants

11. The Airport Operator must _____ access to each air operations area.   11.__

    A. prevent   B. allow   C. forbid
    D. control   E. guard

12. The _____ MOST directly depends on the volume of passenger traffic and the configuration of the terminal screening point.   12.__

    A. response time of the law enforcement officers
    B. number of law enforcement officers
    C. type of security devices required
    D. nature of the law enforcement response
    E. specific form of law enforcement presence

13. One person carrying out both the screening process and the law enforcement function may be an adequate security measure   13.__

    A. when cost is a factor
    B. at certain small airports
    C. at low risk airports
    D. for planes of a certain seating configuration
    E. in no case

14. The training program of law enforcement officers should be based on   14.____

    A. state or local training standards
    B. minimum requirements of basic military training
    C. the broadest spectrum of police duties
    D. uniform FAA standards
    E. the specific needs of the individual airport

15. A weapon found at the airport other than in the screening point, or within a sterile area, is   15.____
subject to

    A. FAA authority   B. highway patrol
    C. local law   D. flight security
    E. federal law

16. A change in _____ would NOT necessitate amending the security program.   16.____

    A. facilities or equipment
    B. an alternate security procedure
    C. law enforcement support
    D. system for maintaining records
    E. none of the above

17. After notification of the proper office of a changed condition affecting security, an amend-   17.____
ment must be submitted for approval

    A. at the same time as notification
    B. within 10 days
    C. within 15 days
    D. within 30 days
    E. within 60 days

18. A proposed security amendment may be approved or   18.____

    A. denied
    B. modified, or denied
    C. modified, or transferred
    D. denied, or transferred
    E. denied, or a "pocket" denial issued

19. The FIRST step in the disposition of a petition for reconsideration of a denied amend-   19.____
ment of a security program is

    A. approval or affirming denial
    B. approval or transfer
    C. modification or affirming denial
    D. affirming denial or transfer
    E. affirming denial or "pocket" denial

20. The FAA notifies the _____ of an amendment it has adopted.   20.____

    A. Regional Director   B. Municipal government
    C. Airport Operator   D. air carriers
    E. Administrator

21. Upon receipt of a petition for reconsideration of an amendment adopted by the FAA, the Regional Director may

    A. rescind or modify the amendment
    B. rescind, modify, or issue the amendment as proposed
    C. rescind, issue as proposed, or transfer the petition
    D. issue as proposed, or transfer the petition
    E. rescind, modify, or transfer the petition

21.__

22. An amendment of a security program by the FAA requiring emergency action ALWAYS contains

    A. a stated period of effectiveness
    B. alternate security procedures
    C. a statement of the reasons for the emergency
    D. the power to deputize persons to arrest for both local and federal offenses
    E. all of the above

22.__

23. Each penetration of an air operations area by an unauthorized person must NOT be

    A. prevented
    B. proved and witnessed
    C. proved and repelled
    D. promptly detected and controlled
    E. prohibited

23.__

24. Which law enforcement officers are exempt from completing a training program?

    A. Local or state policemen
    B. Private law enforcement personnel
    C. Locally deputized law enforcement officers
    D. Persons recently separated from military service
    E. None of the above

24.__

25. The role of airport security is to _____ criminal violence.

    A. prevent   B. control   C. circumvent
    D. detect   E. anticipate

25.__

26. A law enforcement officer must have authority to

    A. arrest on or off duty at the airport
    B. arrest while on duty at the airport
    C. arrest at or off the airport, on or off, duty
    D. arrest while on duty at the airport with a warrant
    E. arrest while, on or off duty at the airport, with or without, a warrant

26.__

27. In addition to meeting standards prescribed by either state or local jurisdiction, the training program for law enforcement officers includes training in

    A. use of firearms
    B. disarming bombs
    C. use of explosives and incendiary devices
    D. bomb detection
    E. undercover support

27.__

4

28. The FAA requires officers' attitudes toward persons subject to aviation security activities to be   28._____

     A. authoritative   B. respectful   C. threatening
     D. courteous   E. understanding

29. The Airport Operator may request the use of additional law enforcement officers when   29._____

     A. they are not available in sufficient numbers
     B. air carrier security over an exclusive area endangers the air operations area
     C. an emergency situation exists
     D. a threat has been received
     E. all of the above

30. Before requesting federal law enforcement officers, the Airport Operator must show   30._____

     A. efforts to recruit additional personnel
     B. efforts to obtain law enforcement from state, local and private agencies
     C. a condition exists preventing use of state, local and private agencies
     D. the inadequacy of state, local and private agencies
     E. that a strike or job action situation exists

31. The cost of federal law enforcement officers used for airport security is the responsibility of the   31._____

     A. FAA
     B. federal agency supplying them
     C. municipal district in which airport is located
     D. air carrier requesting use
     E. Airport Operator

32. Use of law enforcement officers for airport security that are employed by a federal agency other than the FAA requires the consent of the   32._____

     A. Administrator   B. Regional Director
     C. Airport Operator   D. head of that agency
     E. Department of Transportation

33. Federal law enforcement officers used for airport security may be in the employ of   33._____

     A. the FAA
     B. the Treasury Department
     C. the Transportation Department
     D. the Commerce Department
     E. any Federal agency

34. The MINIMUM period of time a record must be maintained is   34._____

     A. 30 days   B. 60 days   C. 90 days   D. 1 year   E. 2 years

35. The airport operator need NOT include in his record   35._____

     A. an actual bombing
     B. the number of real bombs found
     C. simulated bombs found

D. number of threats received
E. none of the above

36. FAA security regulations were originally designed to meet threats   36.__

    A. affecting national security
    B. of terrorist groups
    C. of hijacking
    D. involving carriage of firearms, explosives or incendiary devices
    E. of criminal violence

37. FAA security regulations were originally intended to protect   37.__

    A. commuter air carriers   B. foreign air carriers
    C. larger air terminals   D. route carriers
    E. wholly intrastate air carriers

38. A security program is required of an airplane with a seating configuration of 9 when the   38.__

    A. flight is intrastate
    B. flight is interstate
    C. FAA identifies a security threat
    D. passengers have controlled access to a sterile area
    E. passengers have uncontrolled access to a sterile area

39. The cost of security requirements may be higher for particular flights because of   39.__

    A. scheduling   B. airplane complexity
    C. capacity enplanements   D. vulnerable destinations
    E. limited enplanements

40. The increased security threat to the commuter industry since implementation of the Deregulation Act is a result of the use of   40.__

    A. larger aircraft
    B. scheduled operations
    C. popular routes
    D. public charter operations
    E. there has been no increase

41. Potential hijackers would *most likely* consider   41.__

    A. route and range
    B. range and number of passengers
    C. schedule and destination
    D. route and destination
    E. carrier and destination

42. A general rule applicable to security requirements is that security is commensurate with   42.__

    A. the size of the airport
    B. the number of operations
    C. size of the air operations area
    D. the existing threat
    E. cost

43. A security screening system is required by an operator using airplanes with a seating   43.____
capacity of 40 when

    A.   passengers have uncontrolled access to an exclusive area
    B.   passengers have controlled access to a sterile area
    C.   no antihijacking crew training is available
    D.   the FAA identifies a security threat
    E.   at all times

44. Operators of airplanes may discharge unscreened passengers into a sterile area when   44.____

    A.   their access is controlled through surveillance and escort procedures
    B.   prior arrangement has been made with the FAA
    C.   operators are not required to screen their passengers
    D.   procedures are used to prevent or deter the introduction of explosives and incendi-
       aries into the area
    E.   at no time

45. Deplaning passengers are screened before entry into a sterile area when   45.____

    A.   the airplane is unprotected
    B.   the airplane operator was not previously required to screen them
    C.   law enforcement support is not required
    D.   the baggage claims area is located in a sterile area
    E.   the airport operator requires it

46. Responsibility for establishing and implementing law enforcement arrangements at air-   46.____
ports regularly serving smaller airplanes at which screening is not required is borne by
the

    A.   law enforcement agency   B.   Airport Operator
    C.   Regional Director   D.   airplane operator
    E.   airport security

47. Most of the costs of meeting contingency procedures due to a threat condition are asso-   47.____
ciated with the cost of

    A.   alterations to airport terminals
    B.   metal detectors
    C.   personnel
    D.   x-ray machines
    E.   training programs

48. The MOST frequent cause of a new security cost for the operator of smaller airplanes is   48.____

    A.   meeting threat situations
    B.   the desire to discharge passengers directly into a sterile area
    C.   the desire to operate out of larger airports
    D.   meeting FAA requirements
    E.   the desire to become an FAA certificate holder

49. Interim measures instituted to maintain security under changed conditions remain in effect until 49.___

    A. an amendment to the security program is approved
    B. the FAA security office evaluates the situation
    C. the interim measures are approved
    D. the airport operator conducts his investigation
    E. the FAA security office proposes alternate measures

50. The FAA is authorized to prescribe regulations affecting activity 50.___

    A. in sterile areas
    B. in any area not designated "exclusive"
    C. aboard aircraft
    D. at the airport and aboard aircraft
    E. on areas adjacent to the airport, at the airport, and aboard aircraft

---

KEY (CORRECT ANSWERS)

1. A	11. D	21. E	31. E	41. B
2. A	12. E	22. C	32. D	42. D
3. B	13. B	23. B	33. E	43. D
4. C	14. A	24. E	34. C	44. A
5. B	15. C	25. B	35. E	45. B
6. D	16. D	26. B	36. C	46. D
7. C	17. D	27. A	37. D	47. C
8. E	18. A	28. D	38. E	48. B
9. B	19. B	29. A	39. E	49. A
10. E	20. C	30. B	40. E	50. D

EXAMINATION SECTION
TEST 1

DIRECTIONS: Each question or incomplete statement is followed by several suggested answers or completions. Select the one that BEST answers the question or completes the statement. *PRINT THE LETTER OF THE CORRECT ANSWER IN THE SPACE AT THE RIGHT.*

1. The Airport Administrator may request the use of   1.____

    A. the National Guard
    B. deputized citizens
    C. federal law enforcement officers
    D. military personnel
    E. all of the above

2. Areas used *exclusively* by helicopters are NOT included in the definition of an Air Operations Area becuase they   2.____

    A. are outside FAA authority
    B. do not pose a sufficient threat
    C. are the exclusive responsibility of the operators
    D. do not have sufficient traffic
    E. are considered part of general aviation operations

3. The FAA encouraged the adoption of the Air Carrier Standard Security Program in order to   3.____

    A. ensure uniform implementation and use of security procedures
    B. ensure minimum security to all carriers
    C. ensure efficient and cost effective implementation of security procedures
    D. lessen the administrative burden
    E. reduce the threat of violence among all carriers

4. Implementing documents   4.____

    A. are filed with the airport operator
    B. are filed with the law enforcement agency
    C. are filed with the Regional Director
    D. must be included in the security program
    E. may be appended to the security program

5. The *initial* determination of the adequacy of the security program after a change of condition occurs is made by   5.____

    A. any FAA personnel assigned to inspect the airport
    B. the Regional Director
    C. the Airport Operator
    D. the Law Enforcement Officer noting the changed condition
    E. any inspector in the position of monitoring the program's implementation

6. An air carrier may limit its responsibility within an Air Operation Area to a(n) _____ area.   6.__

    A. exclusive   B. sterile   C. secure
    D. emergency   E. authorized

7. The security program is approved by the   7.__

    A. Airplane Operator   B. Regional Director
    C. law enforcement agency   D. Airport Director
    E. Airport Operator

8. An *exclusive* area differs from that of an Air Operation Area by its   8.__

    A. inclusion of the screening program
    B. inclusion of barrier composition
    C. exclusion of terrain
    D. description of expected use
    E. inclusion of the terms of the agreement establishing the area

9. The security program is available for inspection upon the request of any   9.__

    A. law enforcement officer
    B. air carrier personnel
    C. person traveling in air transportation
    D. Civil Aviation Security Inspector
    E. municipal or state official

10. A petition for reconsideration of approval of a security program must be filed with the   10.__

    A. Regional Director
    B. Civil Aviation Security Inspector
    C. Administrator
    D. Airport Operator
    E. law enforcement agency

11. Coordination of security activities between airport tenants is necessary because   11.__

    A. security in these areas is standardized
    B. security in these areas is the responsibility of the airport operator
    C. these areas affect the security of other areas of the airport
    D. individual facilities and equipment are not adequate to perform the control functions
    E. FAA requires shared responsibility among tenants

12. MOST likely to *increase* security costs to the air carrier is   12.__

    A. airport operators passing on increased costs to them
    B. the need for added patrols, guards and other measures
    C. achieving compatibility with the airport's security program
    D. the loss of security responsibility of the tenants
    E. airport operators requiring them to have security measures beyond those required by the FAA

13. The identification system used for secure areas at small, low-volume airports is: 13.____

    A. Badges with identifying photo
    B. Personal recognition
    C. Code
    D. Voice print
    E. Security key

14. Law requires that law enforcement officers   14.____

    A. be physically located at each screening point
    B. be within sight of each screening point
    C. be within a one minute response time to each screening point
    D. secure specific areas regardless of screening point locations
    E. none of the above

15. The FAA position on the wearing of uniforms by law enforcement officers is: 15.____

    A. A uniform is not advantageous under all circumstances
    B. Uniforms are desirable except when departmental regulations prohibit off-duty policemen from wearing them
    C. Uniforms are the prerogative of the police administrator
    D. Uniforms are essential for public recognition
    E. Uniforms detract from effective law enforcement

16. The FAA rules regarding carriage of firearms, explosives and incendiary devices are NOT a violation of the Second Amendment because   16.____

    A. the Second Amendment does not confer an absolute right to carry weapons at all times and places
    B. the Second Amendment does not allow the endangerment of persons and property
    C. Congress has granted the FAA broad authority
    D. foreign and domestic air carriers have immunity to the Second Amendment
    E. national security supercedes the right conferred by the Amendment

17. BEST qualified to fulfill the record requirement is the   17.____

    A. law enforcement agency   B. Federal Reports Bureau
    C. FAA Security Office   D. Airport Operator
    E. Airplane Operator

18. Notification of a changed condition affecting security must be given   18.____

    A. immediately   B. within 3 days   C. within 7 days
    D. within 15 days   E. within 30 days

19. How many days before the proposed effective date does an amendment of the security program have to be submitted?   19.____

    A. 15   B. 30   C. 45   D. 60   E. 90

20. The most important consideration in approving a proposed amendment of a security program is: 20.___

    A. Efficiency and cost
    B. Local ordinances and individual need
    C. Implementation and effectiveness
    D. Safety and public interest
    E. Uniformity

21. The administrator may amend an approved security program when   21.___

    A. it is determined that safety and public interest require it
    B. the level of security changes
    C. alternate security procedures require it
    D. a complaint is received
    E. a violation occurs

22. A petition for reconsideration stays an amendment adopted by the FAA   22.___

    A. 15 days   B. 30 days
    C. 60 days   D. 90 days
    E. until final action is taken on the petition

23. When there is an emergency requiring immediate action, an amendment may be issued effective on the date of receipt by   23.___

    A. the Administrator or Regional Director
    B. the Airport Operator
    C. any airport carrier or the Airport Operator
    D. the Security Officer
    E. all of the above

24. An Airport Operator is NOT required to provide security control functions over an exclusive area when   24.___

    A. there is written agreement between the air carrier and air operator
    B. there is written approval of the air carrier's security program
    C. the air carrier has exclusive security responsibility
    D. the air carrier's security program conflicts with the airport operator's program
    E. the airport operator's program contains the control function performed by the air carrier and procedures of notification when they are inadequate

25. Law enforcement officers must   25.___

    A. display a badge
    B. carry a badge
    C. wear an identifying insignia
    D. possess an indication of authority
    E. none of the above

26. A law enforcement officer may arrest a suspect for a felony WITHOUT a warrant when he has _____ that the suspect has committed a crime.   26.___

    A. probable cause to believe   B. knowledge   C. proof
    D. suspicion   E. information

27. Law enforcement officers may subject persons to   27._____

    A. search   B. arrest   C. inspection
    D. detention   E. all of the above

28. Training of law enforcement officers in subjects other than those ordinarily prescribed, is   28._____
the prerogative of the

    A. Airport Operator   B. Administrator
    C. Law Enforcement Agency   D. Regional Agency
    E. air carriers

29. The anticipated risk of criminal violence and aircraft piracy at the airport should accom-   29._____
pany requests for

    A. approval of airport security programs
    B. use of interim measures
    C. amending a security program
    D. use of Federal law enforcement officers
    E. use of private law enforcement officers

30. Use of Federal law enforcement officers is intended to _____ state, local and private   30._____
law enforcement officers.

    A. replace   B. assist
    C. supplement   D. reduce the need for
    E. coordinate

31. A record of each law enforcement action is made available to the   31._____

    A. local municipal office where the airport is located
    B. Regional Director
    C. Regional Director upon request
    D. Administrator
    E. Administrator, upon his request

32. The record of firearms, explosives and incendiary devices should include their   32._____

    A. origin
    B. type
    C. hazard potential
    D. all of the above
    E. none of the above

33. No security program is required when the passenger seating configuration is *less* than   33._____

    A. 19   B. 31   C. 49   D. 61   E. 91

34. The security requirement for an airplane with a passenger seating configuration of 35 is: 34._____

    A. No security program required
    B. Airplane and airport operator security program must be adopted
    C. Airplane and airport operator security program must include law enforcement
    D. Airplane and airport operator security program must include screening and law
        enforcement presence
    E. Full security program required

35. All operators are required to

    A. have a security screening system
    B. conduct antihijack crew training
    C. provide law enforcement support
    D. all of the above
    E. none of the above

35.__

36. When an air carrier is required to implement a security screening program, it must also

    A. conduct antihijack crew training
    B. control access to all exclusive areas
    C. provide law enforcement support
    D. adopt a full security program
    E. all of the above

36.__

37. Operators of airplanes may NOT discharge unscreened passengers into a sterile area if the seating configuration EXCEEDS

    A. 19   B. 31   C. 60
    D. 90   E. none of the above

37.__

38. The responsibility of the Airport Operator at airports regularly serving smaller airplanes at which screening of passengers is NOT required is to

    A. ensure the airplane is protected
    B. prevent or deter the introduction of firearms into checked baggage
    C. identify the law enforcement agency chosen for assistance
    D. identify the FAA certificate holder used to screen its passengers
    E. provide surveillance of passengers

38.__

39. When an airplane operator using smaller planes must adopt and carry out a full security program with a screening system, law enforcement support is supplied by the

    A. airplane operator   B. airport security
    C. air carrier   D. FAA certificate holder
    E. Airport Operator

39.__

40. The likelihood of operators of smaller airplanes being required to implement contingency procedures due to a threat situation is rated at *approximately*

    A. 90% or more   B. 70%   C. 50%
    D. 30%   E. 10% or less

40.__

41. The FAA's authority derives from the

    A. Department of Transportation
    B. Civil Aeronautics Board
    C. National Security Act
    D. Department of Justice
    E. Congress

41.__

42. The Air Operations Area excludes areas that are *exclusively* used by   42.____

    A. certificate holders
    B. foreign operators
    C. general aviation operations
    D. helicopters
    E. airport tenants

43. Locally deputized law enforcement officers who do NOT have authority of arrest for   43.____
federal offenses may

    A. arrest for local violations that are comparable to federal violations
    B. be empowered to arrest for federal offenses by the airport operator
    C. be empowered to arrest for federal offenses by the Administrator
    D. arrest for federal violations in areas not designated "sterile"
    E. not be used for airport security

44. The Airport Operator's responsibility is BEST described as: 44.____

    A. To provide for the safety of persons and property traveling in air transportation
    B. To take whatever steps that are necessary to meet all possible security threats
    C. To prevent all acts of criminal violence and aircraft piracy
    D. To ensure no firearm, explosive or incendiary device is introduced aboard any aircraft or sterile area
    E. To provide law enforcement in situations in which the threat of criminal violence and aircraft piracy demand it

45. An air carrier may limit its responsibility within an Air Operations Area by a(n)   45.____

    A. proposed amendment   B. oral understanding
    C. petition   D. approved amendment
    E. written agreement

46. Access is controlled in a sterile area by   46.____

    A. the inspection of persons and property
    B. use of identification media
    C. personal recognition
    D. armed guard
    E. security gates

47. A description of an Air Operations area should include   47.____

    A. dimensions, boundaries and pertinent features
    B. the names of the occupants
    C. the law enforcement agency used, the method of summoning assistance and the training program of the officers
    D. type and seating configuration of all aircraft
    E. emergency exits and other safety features

48. Security regulations for airports prevent tenants from

    A. accepting responsibility for the security of its leased area
    B. carrying out its own security program
    C. involvement in the design and implementation of overall airport security
    D. all of the above
    E. none of the above

48.__

49. An amendment issued WITHOUT a stay is effective upon receipt when

    A. an airport operator requests it
    B. an emergency requires immediate action
    C. the FAA amends a security program
    D. at no time
    E. at all times

49.__

50. All law enforcement officers must be armed

    A. at all times
    B. under any emergency situation
    C. in the presence of the passenger screening system
    D. while on duty on the airport
    E. if local ordinances provide the authority for arming

50.__

KEY (CORRECT ANSWERS)

1. C	11. C	21. A	31. E	41. E
2. B	12. C	22. E	32. B	42. D
3. A	13. B	23. A	33. B	43. A
4. E	14. E	24. E	34. B	44. A
5. C	15. D	25. D	35. B	45. E
6. A	16. A	26. A	36. C	46. A
7. B	17. D	27. E	37. E	47. A
8. E	18. A	28. B	38. C	48. E
9. D	19. B	29. D	39. E	49. B
10. A	20. D	30. C	40. E	50. D

EXAMINATION SECTION
TEST 1

DIRECTIONS: Each question or incomplete statement is followed by several suggested answers or completions. Select the one that BEST answers the question or completes the statement. *PRINT THE LETTER OF THE CORRECT ANSWER IN THE SPACE AT THE RIGHT.*

1. The record of airport law enforcement actions is kept by the   1.____

    A. law enforcement agency
    B. domestic and foreign air carriers
    C. Airport Operator
    D. Regional Director
    E. Security Director

2. Federally-mandated "guards" are empowered to   2.____

    A. enforce only statutes relating to aviation security
    B. enforce Federal law
    C. enforce the criminal law of the State and local jurisdiction
    D. support local law enforcement officers
    E. enforce all laws necessary for safety protection

3. Areas other than Airport Operation Areas that should be identified in the security pro-   3.____
gram are those which

    A. do not pose a specific threat to air carrier operations
    B. are adjacent to the airport
    C. give access to each Airport Operation Area
    D. clearly present a danger to persons and property in the Airport Operation Area
    E. no other area need be identified

4. Those who have access to the airport security program are all   4.____

    A. air carriers served by the airport
    B. FAA personnel
    C. FAA personnel assigned to inspect the airport
    D. airport users
    E. persons who have an operational need-to-know

5. The airport _____ operates an airport that regularly serves holders of certificates of   5.____
scheduled operations.

    A. Enforcement Officer   B. Administrator
    C. Director   D. Operator
    E. Carrier

6. Access is controlled to a(n) _____ area.   6.____

    A. secure   B. exclusive
    C. sterile   D. emergency
    E. air operations

7. The _____ signs and approves the airport security program.　　　　7.__

   A. Administrator　　　　　　　　　　B. Airport Operator
   C. Regional Director　　　　　　　　D. Security Director
   E. individual air carriers

8. The security program should be submitted for approval _____ days before scheduled　　8.__
passenger operations are to begin.

   A. 30　　　　　B. 60　　　　　C. 90　　　　　D. 120　　　　　E. 180

9. Modification of proposed amendments to the security program are *usually* accomplished　　9.__
through

   A. mutual agreement between the Regional Director and the Airport Operator
   B. the Air Transportation Security Field Office
   C. the Regional Director
   D. mutual agreement between the air carriers
   E. mutual agreement between the air carriers and the Airport Operator

10. The _____ is in the BEST position to act as the focal point for the coordination of the　　10.__
security activities between all airport tenants.

   A. private law enforcement　　　　　　B. Security Director
   C. Regional Director　　　　　　　　　D. Airport Operator
   E. Air Carrier/ Tenant Commission

11. Unauthorized persons and ground vehicles should be prevented from entry into each air　　11.__
operations area.
An unauthorized person and ground vehicle is defined as one

   A. whose entry is not approved by the Airport Operator
   B. who the law enforcement officer has reason to believe is a suspect to a crime
   C. who threatens the safety of persons traveling in air transportation
   D. whose entry may be detrimental to the safety of persons traveling in air transportation
   E. who cannot produce the correct identification

12. The BEST deterrent to persons threatening criminal violence is　　12.__

   A. a flexible response system for all law enforcement officers
   B. use of one person carrying out the screening process and the law enforcement
function
   C. law enforcement officer visibility in general
   D. visible presence of a law enforcement officer at each screening point
   E. use of undercover law enforcement officers

13. The cost of law enforcement support is *ultimately* borne by the　　13.__

   A. U.S. Government
   B. passengers
   C. U.S. Government and foreign air carriers
   D. Airport Operators
   E. Civil Aeronautics Board

14. The FAA does NOT prohibit the legal carriage of firearms for sporting purposes when   14.____
those firearms

    A. are legally obtained and licensed
    B. are not accessible to unauthorized persons in a sterile area
    C. are carried without firing power
    D. all of the above
    E. none of the above

15. Records which MUST be kept and logged are those   15.____

    A. which pertain to the immediate disposition of detainees
    B. which apply only to aviation security matters
    C. are obtained by the screening process
    D. of each law enforcement action
    E. of each violation of airport security

16. Any changed condition affecting the security of the airport must be given to the   16.____

    A. Air Transportation Security
    B. Civil Aeronautics Board
    C. FAA Security Office
    D. Federal Aviation Bureau
    E. Department of Transportation

17. A proposed amendment of a security program must be submitted to the   17.____

    A. Airport Operator   B. Administrator
    C. Superintendent   D. Security Officer
    E. Regional Director

18. Automatic approval of proposed amendments of security programs are NOT granted   18.____
after a specific time period because that would

    A. allow air carriers independent action
    B. justify interim measures
    C. not allow for modification
    D. transfer responsibility
    E. not be in the public interest

19. How many days are given to act on a petition for reconsideration of a denied proposed   19.____
amendment of a security program?

    A. 7   B. 10   C. 15
    D. 30   E. no period is specified

20. The effective date for an amendment to a security program adopted by the FAA is not   20.____
less than _____ days after the Airport Operator is in receipt of the notice of amendment.

    A. 10   B. 15
    C. 20   D. 30
    E. upon receipt of the notice of amend-
       ment

21. A display of identification is required within the air operations area   21.___

     A.   when there is an emergency or other unusual condition
     B.   when access needs to be controlled
     C.   when it is appropriate
     D.   at no time
     E.   at all times

22. Law enforcement officers are provided by the   22.___

     A.   local law enforcement agency
     B.   Airport Operator
     C.   Department of Justice
     D.   FAA Security Office
     E.   Federal Law Enforcement Agency

23. All law enforcement officers must be authorized to   23.___

     A.   carry a firearm   B.   issue firearmsi
     C.   carry and use a firear   D.   have access to firarms
     E.   display a firearm

24. The training standards of law enforcement officers, if those prescribed by State and local   24.___
jurisdiction do not apply, is approved by the

     A.   Airport Operator
     B.   Regional Director
     C.   Security Officer
     D.   Airport Operator and Air Carriers
     E.   Administrator

25. The responsibilities of a Law Enforcement Officer are determined by the   25.___

     A.   Department of Justice
     B.   Federal Bureau of Investigation
     C.   Federal Aviation Administration
     D.   Civil Aeronautics Board
     E.   Air Transportation Security

26. The _____ is necessary information for Federal Law Enforcement Officers.   26.___

     A.   number of acts and attempted acts of air piracy
     B.   number of passengers emplaned at the airport
     C.   number of detentions and arrests
     D.   estimated number of persons affected by security
     E.   number of law enforcement officers employed

27. No person, except those authorized, may have a firearm, explosive or incendiary device   27.___

     A.   in a sterile area
     B.   in an exclusive area
     C.   in an airport operations area
     D.   on airport property
     E.   on any area on or adjacent to the airport

28. The number of _____ must be included in the records.   28.____

    A. arrests
    B. persons subjected to inspection
    C. persons searched
    D. persons screened
    E. all of the above

29. The degree of security for commuter carriers and route carriers is comparable when   29.____
commuter carriers

    A. provide substitute service on routes previously served by route carriers
    B. serve the same number of passengers as route carriers
    C. conduct scheduled operations
    D. conduct public charter operations
    E. depart from the same terminals as route carriers

30. A full security program must be adopted and implemented when the passenger seating   30.____
configuration is *more* than

    A. 9   B. 19   C. 31   D. 60   E. 80

31. MOST likely subject to hijacking are   31.____

    A. large, long range airplanes
    B. small, short range airplanes
    C. airplanes operating out of smaller airports
    D. airplanes operating out of larger airports
    E. airplanes with evening departures

32. The MOST important consideration in determining security requirements is the   32.____

    A. carrier   B. route
    C. cost   D. number of passengers
    E. airplane size

33. Some air carriers have voluntarily elected to upgrade their security program in order to 33.____

    A. allow their passengers direct and uncontrolled access to sterile areas
    B. meet passenger expectations
    C. lessen administrative burdens
    D. gain landing privileges at larger airports
    E. become an FAA Certificate Holder

34. A security program that does NOT require screening of passengers must include all the   34.____
following EXCEPT:

    A. The law enforcement support available upon request
    B. The established response time of the support
    C. A description of the procedure to summon support
    D. A description of the training of the law enforcement support
    E. A description of the system of records of law enforcement actions taken in support
       of aviation security

35. To ensure adequate, efficient and cost-effective implementation of contingency procedures, the affected airplane operators may seek help from

    A. Air Transportation Security
    B. Civil Aeronautics Board
    C. Federal Aviation Administration
    D. Department of Transportation
    E. Office of Management and Budget

35.___

36. Authorized to prescribe regulations affecting the safety of passengers is the

    A. Airplane Operator   B. Administrator
    C. Regional Director   D. Airport Operator
    E. air carrier

36.___

37. Arrest power for employees of private security forces is conferred by

    A. Congress   B. State statutes
    C. the FAA   D. the Airport Operator
    E. the private security force

37.___

38. Locally deputized law enforcement officers need NOT have authority to

    A. search suspects   B. detain suspects
    C. use firearms   D. arrest for local offenses
    E. arrest for federal offenses

38.___

39. All of the following must be inlcuded in the security program EXCEPT:

    A. The number of passengers enplaned at the airport during the preceding calendar year
    B. The procedures, and a description of the facilities and equipment used for security
    C. A description of the law enforcement support
    D. A description of the system for maintaining records
    E. A description of the training program for law enforcement officers

39.___

40. Security programs are based upon the security needs of

    A. general aviation areas
    B. air carriers
    C. an entire, specifically defined area
    D. individual elements within the area of control
    E. threatened areas

40.___

41. The security of an *exclusive* area is the responsibility of the

    A. Airport Operator
    B. air carrier tenant
    C. private law enforcement
    D. Airport Operator and air carrier tenant
    E. Airport Operator and private law enforcement,

41.___

42. The suggested MAXIMUM response time of law enforcement support is _____ minute(s).

    A. 1   B. 2   C. 3-5   D. 5-7   E. 7-10

42.___

43. The decision as to what law enforcement presence is adequate is the responsibility of the

    A. Airport Operator   B. Regional Director
    C. Administrator   D. Congress
    E. State

43.____

44. The design and style of a law enforcement uniform should identify the wearer as a(n)

    A. airport employee   B. soldier
    C. police officer   D. government employee
    E. official

44.____

45. Accurate information relating to the operation of the civil aviation security program is essential in order to

    A. protect passenger rights
    B. determine future budgets
    C. comply with public disclosure laws
    D. meet local ordinances
    E. evaluate its effectiveness

45.____

46. The Airport Operator's responsibility concerning a changed condition affecting security is to

    A. determine how security may be compromised
    B. effect interim measures
    C. submit an appropriate amendment for approval
    D. apply to the FAA for an emergency procedure
    E. increase law enforcement support

46.____

47. Approval or disapproval of a proposed amendment of a security program must be given within _____ days after receipt.

    A. 7   B. 10   C. 15   D. 30   E. 60

47.____

48. A petition for reconsideration of a denied amendment of a security program must be filed with the

    A. Superintendent   B. Security Officer
    C. Regional Director   D. Administrator
    E. Airport Operator

48.____

49. Response to a notice of a FAA proposed amendment is fixed by the FAA as

    A. not less than 15 days   B. not less than 30 days
    C. not less than 60 days   D. not more than 15 days
    E. not more than 30 days

49.____

50. Final action on a petition for reconsideration of an amendment adopted by the FAA is made by the

    A. Administrator   B. Security Officer
    C. Regional Director   D. Review Board
    E. Airport Operator

50.____

KEY (CORRECT ANSWERS)

1.	C	11.	A	21.	C	31.	A	41.	B
2.	E	12.	D	22.	B	32.	E	42.	A
3.	D	13.	B	23.	C	33.	A	43.	C
4.	E	14.	B	24.	E	34.	B	44.	C
5.	D	15.	D	25.	C	35.	C	45.	E
6.	C	16.	C	26.	B	36.	B	46.	B
7.	B	17.	E	27.	A	37.	B	47.	C
8.	C	18.	E	28.	A	38.	E	48.	C
9.	A	19.	E	29.	A	39.	A	49.	B
10.	D	20.	D	30.	D	40.	C	50.	A

DIRECTIONS: Each question or incomplete statement is followed by several suggested answers or completions. Select the one the BEST answers the question or completes the statement. *PRINT THE LETTER OF THE CORRECT ANSWER IN THE SPACE AT THE RIGHT.*

1. Officer Hayes has arrived at the scene of an automobile accident to find the two drivers arguing heatedly in the middle of the intersection, where their two cars remain entangled by their front bumpers. Traffic has backed up on all four sides of the intersection. As Officer Hayes approaches, the two drivers each begin to tell their side of the story at the same time. As they grow more agitated and begin to call each other names, one of the drivers threatens the other with physical harm. In this situation, Officer Hayes' first action should be to

   A. ask each driver to stand on an opposite corner of the intersection and wait for him to begin documenting the accident
   B. call a tow truck to clear the accident from the intersection
   C. arrest the driver who made the threat
   D. ask the drivers to pull their cars out of the intersection and off to the side of the road

1.____

2. Probably the most important thing a police officer can do to build and strengthen a trusting relationship with community members is to

   A. patrol the area often and conspicuously
   B. listen to them in a respectful and nonjudgemental way
   C. make sure people understand his background and qualifications
   D. establish clear, reachable goals for improving the community

2.____

3. Which of the following is NOT a factor that should influence an officer's exercise of discretion?

   A. Clear statutes and protocols
   B. Informal expectations of legislatures and the public
   C. Use of force
   D. Limited resources

3.____

4. The term for the policing style which emphasizes order maintenance is _____ style.

   A. service
   B. coercive
   C. watchman
   D. legalistic

4.____

5. Officer Torres, a community service law enforcement officer, approaches the home of recent Vietnamese immigrants to speak to several community members gathered there. He notices several pairs of shoes on the front porch. It is reasonable for Officer Torres to assume that

   A. the people in the home are superstitious
   B. the house must have some religious significance

5.____

C. if he removes his own shoes before entering, it will be perceived as a sign of respect

D. the homeowners are having their carpets cleaned

6. Ethical issues are   6.___

   A. usually a problem only in individual behaviors
   B. relevant to all aspects of police work
   C. usually referred to a board or committee for decision-making
   D. the same as legal issues

7. In using the "reflection of meaning" technique in a client interview, a social worker should   7.___
    do each of the following, EXCEPT

   A. Begin with a sentence stem such as "You mean..." or "Sounds like you believe..."
   B. Offer an interpretation of the client's words.
   C. Add paraphrasing of longer client statements.
   D. Close with a "check-out" such as, "Am I hearing you right?"

8. A police officer is speaking with a victim who is hearing-impaired. The police officer   8.___
    should try to do each of the following, EXCEPT

   A. speak slowly and clearly
   B. gradually increase the volume of his voice
   C. face the victim squarely
   D. reduce or eliminate any background or ambient noise

9. An officer is interviewing a witness who is a recent immigrant from China. In general, the   9.___
    officer should avoid

   A. verbal tracking or requests for clarification
   B. open-ended questions
   C. sustained eye contact
   D. attentive body language

10. Which of the following statements about rape is FALSE?   10.___

   A. The use of alcohol and drugs can reduce sexual inhibitions.
   B. Rape is a crime of violence.
   C. Rape is a crime that can only be committed against women.
   D. It is not a sustainable legal charge if the partner has already consented to sex in
        the past.

11. A person's individual code of ethics is typically determined by each of the following fac-   11.___
    tors, EXCEPT

   A. reason
   B. religion
   C. emotion
   D. law

12. Officer Long, new to the urban precinct where he is assigned patrol, has received a pair   12.____
of complaints from two customers about the owner of a local convenience store, who
works the cash register on most days. According to one customer, the owner became
angry and ordered her out of the store after she had asked the price of a certain item.
The other customer claims that on another occasion, the owner pulled a handgun from
behind the counter and trained it on him as he walked slowly out of the store with his
hands up. Each of the customers has lived in the neighborhood for many years and has
never before seen or heard of any strange behavior on the owner's part.
In investigating these complaints, Officer Long should suspect that

     A.   the owner should be considered armed and dangerous, and any entry into the
store should be made with weapons drawn
     B.   the cause of the problem is most likely the onset of a serious psychological distur-
bance
     C.   the customers may have reasons to be untruthful about the convenience store
owner
     D.   the store owner has probably experienced a recent trauma, such as a robbery
attempt or a personal loss

13. Typical signs and symptoms of stress include   13.____
        I.   weakened immune system
       II.   prolonged, vivid daydreams
      III.   insomnia
      IV.   depression

     A.   I only
     B.   I, III and IV
     C.   III and IV
     D.   I, II, III and IV

14. Other than solid, ethical police work, an officer's best defense against a lawsuit or com-   14.____
plaint is usually

     A.   detailed case records
     B.   a capable advocate
     C.   a vigorous counterclaim against the plaintiff
     D.   the testimony of professional character witnesses

15. Assertive people   15.____

     A.   avoid stating feelings, opinions, or desires
     B.   appear passive, but behave aggressively
     C.   state their views and needs directly
     D.   appear aggressive, but behave passively

16. In the non-verbal communication process, meaning is most commonly provided by   16.____

     A.   body language
     B.   touch
     C.   tone of voice
     D.   context

17. The most obvious practical benefit that deviance has on a society is the 17.____

    A. advancement of the status quo
    B. vindication of new laws
    C. inducement to reach cultural goals
    D. promotion of social unity

18. What is the term for policing that focuses on providing a wider and more thorough array 18.____
of social services to defeat the social problems that cause crime?

    A. Reflective policing
    B. Order maintenance
    C. Social engineering
    D. Holistic policing

19. The term "active listening" mostly refers to a person's ability to 19.____

    A. both listen and accomplish other tasks at the same time
    B. take an active role in determining which information is provided by the speaker
    C. concentrate on what is being said
    D. indicate with numerous physical cues that he/she is listening

20. Police officers in any jurisdiction are most likely to receive calls about 20.____

    A. threats
    B. suspicious persons
    C. petty theft or property crime
    D. disturbances, such as family arguments

21. Which of the following is NOT a physiological explanation for rape? 21.____

    A. uncontrollable sex drive
    B. lack of available partners
    C. reaction to repressed desires
    D. consequence of the natural selection process.

22. Which of the following is an element of self-discipline? 22.____

    A. Establishing and reaching short-term goals
    B. Establishing and reaching long-term goals
    C. Taking an honest look at one's lifestyle and making conscious changes toward improvement
    D. Taking an honest look at one's personality and revealing traits, both good and bad, to others

23. Most of the events in a person's life are the result of 23.____

    A. chance events
    B. a sense of intuition
    C. individual choices and decisions
    D. the decisions of one's parents or other authority figures

24. Which of the following is the most effective way for a department to limit the discretion exercised by police officers?   24.____

    A. Open and flexible departmental directives
    B. Close supervision by departmental management
    C. Broadening role definitions for officers.
    D. Statutory protection from civil liability lawsuits

25. Police officers who demonstrate critical thinking skills are also more likely to demonstrate each of the following, EXCEPT   25.____

    A. the ability to empathize
    B. the tendency to criticize
    C. self-awareness
    D. reflective thinking

KEY (CORRECT ANSWERS)

1.	A		11.	D
2.	B		12.	D
3.	A		13.	B
4.	C		14.	A
5.	C		15.	C
6.	B		16.	A
7.	B		17.	D
8.	B		18.	D
9.	C		19.	C
10.	D		20.	D

21.	C
22.	C
23.	C
24.	B
25.	B

29

TEST 2

DIRECTIONS: Each question or incomplete statement is followed by several suggested answers or completions. Select the one the BEST answers the question or completes the statement. *PRINT THE LETTER OF THE CORRECT ANSWER IN THE SPACE AT THE RIGHT.*

1. Officer Park responds to a domestic disturbance call to find a mother and her two young children huddled together in the living room, all of them crying. The mother explains that her husband is no longer there; he flew into a fit of rage and then stormed out to join his friends for a night of drinking. Officer Park's first action would most likely be to

    A. determine the location of the husband
    B. contact the appropriate social services agency, to arrange a consultation
    C. try to calm the family down and ask the mother to explain what happened
    D. refer the mother to a local battered-spouse shelter

1.____

2. Most commonly, the reason for crimes involving stranger violence is

    A. anger
    B. retaliation
    C. hate
    D. robbery

2.____

3. For a police officer, "burst stress" is most likely to be caused by

    A. a shootout
    B. financial troubles
    C. departmental politics
    D. substance abuse

3.____

4. The most significant factor in whether a person achieves success in his/her personal life, school, and career is

    A. intelligence
    B. a positive attitude
    C. existing financial resources
    D. innate ability

4.____

5. Typically, a professional code of ethics

    A. embodies a broad picture of expected moral conduct.
    B. is voluntary
    C. provides specific guidance for performance in situations
    D. are decided by objective ethicists outside of the profession

5.____

6. Components recognized by contemporary society as elements of sexual harassment include
      I. abuse of power
     II. immature behavior
    III. sexual desire
    IV. hormonal imbalance

6.____

A. I only
B. I and III
C. II and III
D. I, II, III and IV

7. The phrase "substance abuse" is typically defined as   7.____

   A. an addiction to an illegal substance
   B. the continued use of a psychoactive substance even after it creates problems in a person's life
   C. the overuse of an illegal substance
   D. a situation in which a person craves a drug and organizes his or her life around obtaining it

8. The humanist perspective of behavior holds that people who commit crimes or otherwise act badly are   8.____

   A. willfully disregarding societal norms
   B. reacting to the deprivation of basic needs
   C. suffering from a psychological illness
   D. experiencing a moral lapse

9. Which of the following is NOT involved in the process of empathic listening?   9.____

   A. actually hearing exactly what the other person is saying
   B. searching for the "hidden meanings" behind statements
   C. listening without judgement
   D. communicating that you're hearing what the other person is saying, both verbally and nonverbally

10. Which of the following is NOT a component in developing a stress-resistant lifestyle?   10.____

   A. Finding leisure time
   B. Eating nutritious foods
   C. Getting enough sleep
   D. Seeking financial independence

11. Which of the following was NOT a factor that led to the expansion of a community policing model?   11.____

   A. Information obtained at a crime scene during a preliminary investigation was the most important factor determining the probability of an arrest.
   B. Police response times typically had little to do with the probability of making an arrest.
   C. Traditional "preventive patrols" generally failed to reduce crime.
   D. People who knew police officers personally often tried to take advantage of them.

12. Most of the correspondence in a pyramid scheme that has defrauded several elderly victims has been traced to a post office box in a rural area. Probably the simplest and most efficient way of arresting the suspect(s) in this case would be to   12.____

A.   use an elderly man as a "victim" to lure the suspects into an attempt to defraud him
B.   address a letter to the post office box asking the user to come in for questioning
C.   check Postal Service records to see who is leasing the post office box
D.   physically observe the post office box for a while, to see who is using it

13.   The process of hiring a police officer typically involves each of the following, EXCEPT   13.___

A.   technical preparation
B.   medical examination
C.   background checks
D.   physical ability test

14.   The most common form of rape is _____ rape.   14.___

A.   stranger
B.   acquaintance
C.   sadistic rape
D.   spousal rape

15.   Officer Stevens and his partner respond to a domestic disturbance call involving a father   15.___
and his teenage daughter. As the officers arrive at their home, the two are still arguing
heatedly, but when the officers enter, the daughter retreats to the kitchen, where she continues crying. The father explains that his wife, the daughter's mother, died last year, and
the daughter's behavior and school performance have suffered as a result. The father is
afraid that the daughter is falling in with the wrong crowd, and may be getting involved
with drugs. He is afraid for her and doesn't know what to do.
Within the scope of his police role, the most appropriate action for Officer Stevens to
take in this case would be to

A.   warn both the father and the daughter of the potential consequences of conviction
on a charge of disturbing the peace
B.   refer the father and the daughter to a social services or counseling agency
C.   inform the daughter of the drug statutes that may apply in her case as a way to
influence her choices
D.   question the daughter about her feelings surrounding the death of her mother

16.   During an interview, a suspect confesses to the rape of a co-worker that occurred in the   16.___
office after the rest of the employees had left for the day. The suspect says he was tor-
mented by the seductive behavior of the co-worker until he could no longer stand it. He
was himself a victim, he says. In this case, the suspect is making use of the psychological defense mechanism known as

A.   projection
B.   regression
C.   denial
D.   sublimation

17.   Which of the following is NOT a good stress-reduction strategy?   17.___

A.   Spend some time each day doing absolutely nothing
B.   Become more assertive
C.   Develop a hobby
D.   Have a sense of humor

18. The term for the policing style which emphasizes problem-solving is _____ style.   18._____

    A. watchman
    B. order maintenance
    C. service
    D. legalistic

19. According to current rules and statutes, any employer   19._____

    A. may inquire as to a job applicant's age or date of birth
    B. may keep on file information regarding an employee's race, color, religion, sex, or national origin.
    C. may refuse employment to someone without a car
    D. must give a woman who has taken time off for maternity leave her same job and salary when she is ready to return to work

20. During a conversation with the mother of a teenage boy who has been arrested twice for shoplifting, an officer attempts to be an active listener as the mother explains why she thinks the boy is having so much trouble. Being an active listener includes each of the following strategies, EXCEPT   20._____

    A. putting the speaker at ease
    B. interrupting with questions to clarify meaning
    C. summarizing the speaker's major ideas and feelings
    D. withholding criticism

21. Which of the following is NOT a characteristic of the typical poverty-class family?   21._____

    A. Female-headed, single-parent families
    B. Unwed parents
    C. Isolated from neighbors and relatives
    D. High divorce rates

22. When speaking with community members about improving the quality of life in the neighborhood, an officer should look for signs of social desirability bias among the people with whom he's talking. Social desirability bias often causes people to   22._____

    A. judge other people based on their social role rather than inner character
    B. attribute their successes to skill, while blaming external factors for failures
    C. modify their interactions or behaviors based on what they think is acceptable to others
    D. contend for leadership positions

23. For a number of reasons, Officer Stone thinks a fellow officer might have a drinking problem, and decides to talk to her about it. The officer says she doesn't have a drinking problem; she doesn't even take a drink until after it gets dark. Her answer indicates that she   23._____

    A. doesn't have a drinking problem
    B. is probably a social drinker
    C. drinks more during the winter months
    D. is in denial

24. Factors which shape the police role include each of the following, EXCEPT   24.__

    A.   individual goals
    B.   role expectations
    C.   role acquisition
    D.   multiple-role phenomenon

25. "Deviance" is a social term denoting   25.__

    A.   any violation of norms
    B.   any serious violation of norms
    C.   a type of nonconforming behavior recognizable in all cultures
    D.   a specific set of crime statistics

KEY (CORRECT ANSWERS)

1.	C		11.	D
2.	D		12.	D
3.	A		13.	A
4.	B		14.	B
5.	A		15.	B
6.	A		16.	A
7.	B		17.	A
8.	B		18.	C
9.	B		19.	B
10.	D		20.	B

21.	C
22.	C
23.	D
24.	A
25.	A

EXAMINATION SECTION
TEST 1

DIRECTIONS: Each question or incomplete statement is followed by several suggested answers or completions. Select the one that BEST answers the question or completes the statement. *PRINT THE LETTER OF THE CORRECT ANSWER IN THE SPACE AT THE RIGHT.*

1. An indictment is a   1.____

   A. formal charge
   B. overdue payment
   C. bill of particulars relating to a dispute
   D. felony

2. In a trial, a hostile witness is a(n) _____ witness.   2.____

   A. controversial   B. unfriendly
   C. combative   D. evasive

3. Which of the following was an event from 1999 that may reduce the number of guns in   3.____
   this country?

   A. The passage of a strict gun law in Congress
   B. Gun shows were restricted by Congress
   C. The Colt Corporation restricted the sale of its guns
   D. An embargo was placed on guns coming into this country

4. In the state, headlights should be used when visibility is equal to a minimum or less than   4.____
   _____ feet.

   A. 500   B. 750   C. 1,000   D. 1,250

5. You are required to dim your headlights when an approaching vehicle is within _____   5.____
   feet of your vehicle.

   A. 500   B. 400   C. 300   D. 200

6. *Some features of the arrangement of contents in the following pages may perplex some*   6.____
   readers.
   The word *perplex*, as used in the above sentence, means MOST NEARLY

   A. interest   B. enlighten
   C. turnoff   D. confuse

7. Hearsay evidence means   7.____

   A. false evidence
   B. evidence that needs to be verified
   C. it is generally not admissible in court
   D. the person testifying is unsure of its truth

Questions 8-9.

DIRECTIONS: Questions 8 and 9 refer to the following paragraph.

The variations in report writing range from such picayune details as using A.M. or a.m. to more substantive issues as the inclusion or omission of a report summary in the first paragraph.

8.   In the above paragraph, the word *picayune* means MOST NEARLY   8.___

    A.   grammatic   B.   debatable
    C.   trivial   D.   tendentious

9.   In the above paragraph, the word *substantive* means MOST NEARLY   9.___

    A.   cursory   B.   meaningless
    C.   critical   D.   substantial

10.   In accordance with the driver's manual issued by the state, you must report an accident   10.___
when damage is _____ or more.

    A. $500   B. $1,000   C. $1,500   D. $2,000

11.   It is easier to pass a heavy truck on a highway   11.___

    A.   when the roadway is level
    B.   when going uphill
    C.   when going downhill
    D.   on a concrete pavement

12.   In most states, motorcyclists are required to use   12.___

    A.   headlights and taillights only after sundown
    B.   headlights and taillights at all times
    C.   taillights only during daylight hours
    D.   headlights only during daylight hours

13.   DNA refers to   13.___

    A.   a person who dies upon arriving at a hospital
    B.   genetic material
    C.   a chemical reaction
    D.   a powerful drug

14.   An odometer measures the _____ an automobile.   14.___

    A.   speed of
    B.   velocity of
    C.   distance traveled by
    D.   revolutions per second of the engine of

15.   *Profiling has recently become a controversial issue in police work.*   15.___
Profiling, as used in the above sentence, relates to paying special attention to

    A.   a recognizable class of people
    B.   people of low income

C. people who exceed the speed limits
D. the class of people who drive expensive cars

16. Most highways have a minimum speed of _____ MPH.   16._____

    A. 40   B. 35   C. 30   D. 25

17. The lowest automobile accident rate occurs in the _____ year age group.   17._____

    A. 20 to 35   B. 35 to 50   C. 50 to 65   D. 65 to 80

18. *Writing is characterized as narrative description, exposition, and argument.*   18._____
    Exposition, as used in the above sentence, means MOST NEARLY

    A. describing the circumstances of the situation
    B. the explanation of a piece of information
    C. explaining your conclusions
    D. giving the pros and cons of a conclusion

19. A report states that the latent prints have been sent to the laboratory. The word *latent,* as   19._____
    used in the above statement, means MOST NEARLY

    A. missing   B. visible   C. hidden   D. damaged

20. After being *acquitted* in the first trial, O.J. Simpson faced a second trial. The second trial   20._____
    was not double jeopardy because

    A. evidence was withheld from the jury
    B. he was tried on different criminal charges
    C. the second trial was a civil trial
    D. the first trial was against the weight of the evidence

21. To *loiter* means MOST NEARLY to   21._____

    A. gather in a group of five or more
    B. create suspicion of wrongdoing while hanging around
    C. obstruct pedestrian movement
    D. linger in an aimless way

22. The minimum automobile insurance required for property damage in New York State is   22._____

    A. $3,000   B. $5,000   C. $10,000   D. $20,000

23. The maximum speed limit in a village or town is usually _____ MPH.   23._____

    A. 20   B. 25   C. 30   D. 40

24. The purpose of the *two second rule* in driving is to   24._____

    A. give you enough time to stop if there is a traffic signal ahead
    B. give you enough clearance to cut into another lane when passing a car
    C. keep enough room between your vehicle and the one ahead
    D. provide enough room when entering a highway

25. In most states, you may be arrested for driving with a blood alcohol content of _____   25. ___
   percent or more.

   A. .05   B. .10   C. .15   D. .20

KEY (CORRECT ANSWERS)

1.	A		11.	B
2.	B		12.	B
3.	C		13.	B
4.	C		14.	C
5.	A		15.	A
6.	D		16.	A
7.	C		17.	B
8.	C		18.	B
9.	D		19.	C
10.	B		20.	C

21.	D
22.	B
23.	C
24.	C
25.	B

TEST 2

DIRECTIONS: Each question or incomplete statement is followed by several suggested answers or completions. Select the one that BEST answers the question or completes the statement. *PRINT THE LETTER OF THE CORRECT ANSWER IN THE SPACE AT THE RIGHT.*

1. A yellow sign showing two children in black indicates a school crossing. The shape of the sign is a   1.____

    A. square   B. rectangle   C. hexagon   D. pentagon

2. Personal vehicles driven by volunteer firefighters responding to alarms are allowed to display _____ lights.   2.____

    A. blue   B. green   C. red   D. amber

3. The color amber is closest to   3.____

    A. green   B. yellow   C. purple   D. blue

4. Larceny in the legal sense means   4.____

    A. the unlawful taking away of another person's property without his consent
    B. overcharging another person who is making a purchase
    C. deceiving another person as to the value of an item he wishes to purchase
    D. adding a service charge to an agreed price to an item that is purchased

5. A misdemeanor in law refers to   5.____

    A. a financial dispute between two litigants
    B. a minor offense
    C. a burglary where a small amount of goods was stolen
    D. unruly behavior in public

6. An overt act means MOST NEARLY a(n)   6.____

    A. foolish act   B. act done publicly
    C. illegal act   D. outrageous act

7. A defense lawyer works for a client *pro bono*. This means he   7.____

    A. gets paid only if he wins the case
    B. gets paid a fixed fee
    C. works for free
    D. represents his client at half his usual fee

8. Corpus delicti refers to the   8.____

    A. missing person   B. murderer
    C. scene of the crime   D. dead victim

9. The shape of a stop sign is   9.____

    A. triangular   B. square
    C. six-sided   D. eight-sided

10. Service signs are _____ with white letters and symbols.   10.___

    A. blue   B. green   C. yellow   D. red

11. Destination signs are _____ with white letters and symbols.   11.___

    A. blue   B. green   C. yellow   D. red

12. According to the driver's manual, you are prohibited from passing if you cannot safely return to the right lane before any approaching vehicle comes within _____ feet of your car.   12.___

    A. 100   B. 150   C. 200   D. 250

13. When parking near a hydrant, you must be clear of the hydrant a minimum distance of _____ feet.   13.___

    A. 5   B. 10   C. 15   D. 20

14. When parking your vehicle between two parked vehicles, you must park a maximum of _____ inches from the curb.   14.___

    A. 12   B. 15   C. 18   D. 21

15. In order to insure approval, the framers of the Constitution agreed to add a series of amendments after approval to protect people's rights.
The number of amendments that were added is   15.___

    A. six   B. eight   C. ten   D. twelve

16. The amendment number that insures a person's right to bear arms is   16.___

    A. one   B. two   C. three   D. five

17. The amendment number that prevents a person from incriminating himself is   17.___

    A. one   B. three   C. five   D. seven

18. The right of a person to be secure in his house, and against unreasonable search is amendment number   18.___

    A. two   B. four   C. six   D. eight

19. The right of people to assemble peaceably is amendment number   19.___

    A. one   B. two   C. three   D. four

20. 90 kilometers per hour is equivalent to _____ MPH.   20.___

    A. 40   B. 45   C. 50   D. 55

21. A commercial driver's license is required if the vehicle being driven has a gross weight rating of equal to or more than _____ pounds.   21.___

    A. 24,000   B. 26,000   C. 28,000   D. 30,000

22. One kilogram is equivalent to _____ pounds.   22.___

    A. 2.2   B. 2.4   C. 2.6   D. 2.8

23. Failing to stop for a school bus in New York State is worth _____ points on your license. 23.____

    A. 3   B. 4   C. 5   D. 6

24. In the state, the minimum liability insurance required against the death of one person is 24.____

    A. $30,000   B. $50,000   C. $100,000   D. $150,000

25. Before a person is arrested, he is read a statement by the arresting officer. The name 25.____
associated with this procedure is

    A. Megan   B. Zenger   C. Scott   D. Miranda

KEY (CORRECT ANSWERS)

1. D		11. B	
2. A		12. C	
3. B		13. C	
4. A		14. A	
5. B		15. C	
6. B		16. B	
7. C		17. C	
8. D		18. B	
9. D		19. A	
10. A		20. D	

21. B
22. A
23. C
24. B
25. D

TEST 3

DIRECTIONS: Each question or incomplete statement is followed by several suggested answers or completions. Select the one that BEST answers the question or completes the statement. *PRINT THE LETTER OF THE CORRECT ANSWER IN THE SPACE AT THE RIGHT.*

1. In legal terms, a deposition is

   A. a statement made by a person in open court
   B. a statement under oath, but not in open court
   C. the testimony made by a defendant under oath in open court
   D. a statement under oath that is mainly hearsay

   1._

2. In an automobile accident, first check to see if the injured person is breathing. If not, apply

   A. MPR   B. IBR   C. FHR   D. CPR

   2._

3. Hazard vehicles, such as snow plows and tow trucks, display _____ -colored lights.

   A. blue   B. green   C. amber   D. red

   3._

4. The hand signal shown at the right indicates
   A. caution because there is an obstruction ahead
   B. a right turn
   C. a left turn
   D. a stop

   4._

5. A felony is a

   A. crime only where someone is murdered
   B. major crime
   C. crime only where someone is injured
   D. crime only where major physical damage occurs

   5._

6. *Embezzlement* means MOST NEARLY

   A. deceiving   B. the hiding of funds
   C. stealing   D. investing illegally

   6._

7. The writer should be wary of using an entire paragraph for information, while necessary is not really of great importance.
   The word *wary* in the above sentence means MOST NEARLY

   A. uncertain   B. cautious
   C. certain   D. serious

   7._

8. Hearsay evidence is evidence that

   A. is usually admissible in court
   B. can be inferred from preceding evidence
   C. is based on what another person said out of court
   D. is implied in the testimony of a witness

   8._

9. *Excessive bail shall not be required* is amendment number   9._____

    A. two   B. four   C. six   D. eight

10. The writ of habeas corpus is used to   10._____

    A. insure a defendant receives a fair trial
    B. insure a defendant's Fifth Amendment rights
    C. reduce or eliminate bail
    D. prevent a person from being detained illegally

11. The number of justices in the United States Supreme Court is   11._____

    A. 6   B. 7   C. 8   D. 9

12. The *blue wall* refers to law enforcement officers who   12._____

    A. do not publicly condemn fellow officers regardless of facts
    B. set up roadblocks
    C. support their superiors
    D. do their utmost to improve their image

13. The difference between burglary and robbery is   13._____

    A. burglary is breaking into a building to commit theft, while robbery is the use of violence in taking property from a person
    B. the money value taken in a burglary is less than $10,000, whereas in a robbery the money value taken is more than $10,000
    C. burglary takes place at night, whereas robbery takes place in the daytime
    D. burglary takes place indoors, whereas robbery takes place outdoors

14. The Federal government announced new guidelines relating to automobiles. These standards relate to   14._____

    A. automobile weight   B. gas mileage requirements
    C. car infant seats   D. bumper heights

15. General Motors was involved in a famous lawsuit relating to the Chevy Corvair based on   15._____

    A. its crashworthiness
    B. faulty design of the brake system
    C. failure of the transmissions
    D. location of the gas tanks

16. State legislatures are considering restrictions on the use of cellular phones while driving an automobile. The main argument for the restrictions is that   16._____

    A. driving with one hand is hazardous
    B. conversations on the phone are a distraction
    C. cellular phones interfere with the ignition system
    D. the driver is unlikely to hear sirens or hornblowing

17. *Much of their business involves the unpredictable and the bizarre.*   17._____
The word *bizarre*, as used in the above statement, means MOST NEARLY

    A. weird   B. routine
    C. complicated   D. life-threatening

18. *The federal government seized 145 metric tons of cocaine coming into the United States from South America.*
A metric ton is equal to _____ pounds.

    A. 1,800   B. 2,000   C. 2,200   D. 2,400

18.__

19. A kilogram is most nearly _____ pounds.

    A. 2.0   B. 2.2   C. 2.4   D. 2.6

19.__

20. A narcotic drug used in medicine, but less habit-forming than morphine, is

    A. cocaine   B. methadone   C. LSD   D. heroin

20.__

21. Of the following, the one that is a hazard for the large recreational vehicles is

    A. their inability to meet the emission requirements
    B. their bumper height above the ground does not match the height of the bumpers on the smaller-sized vehicles
    C. because the driver is high above the ground, his ability to see his surroundings is impaired
    D. because of the high center of gravity of the recreational vehicles, they become unstable at high speeds

21.__

22. State inspection procedures on emissions focus on

    A. hydrocarbons and CO_2 B. CO and CO_2
    C. SO_2 and CO   D. hydrocarbons and CO

22.__

23. *In order to bring a case before a Grand Jury, the prosecutor must present a prima facie case of guilt before the Grand Jury.*
Prima facie in the above statement means MOST NEARLY

    A. overwhelming evidence to convict
    B. sufficient to convict unless rebutted by the defense
    C. possibly sufficient to convict by an objective jury
    D. with additional evidence would be sufficient to convict

23.__

24. The KKK was denied a permit to hold a parade in New York City. The Klan sued in court claiming a violation of their rights under the _____ Amendment.

    A. First   B. Third   C. Fifth   D. Eighth

24.__

25. In a jury trial for a felony, a jury of twelve must have

    A. a majority decision
    B. 9 members finding the defendant guilty
    C. 11 members finding the defendant guilty
    D. a unanimous finding of guilt

25.__

———————

KEY (CORRECT ANSWERS)

1. B
2. D
3. C
4. D
5. B

6. C
7. B
8. C
9. D
10. D

11. D
12. A
13. A
14. C
15. D

16. B
17. A
18. C
19. B
20. B

21. B
22. D
23. B
24. A
25. D

TEST 4

DIRECTIONS: Each question or incomplete statement is followed by several suggested answers or completions. Select the one that BEST answers the question or completes the statement. *PRINT THE LETTER OF THE CORRECT ANSWER IN THE SPACE AT THE RIGHT.*

1. State law defines a juvenile as _____ years of age or less.   1.___

   A. 15   B. 16   C. 17   D. 18

2. A writ of habeas corpus is an order to   2.___

   A. dismiss charges against a detained person
   B. reduce the charges against a detained person
   C. have a detained person confront his accusors
   D. have a detained person brought before a court

3. A person is brought into a police station to face charges. The person brought in when   3.___
   interrogated refuses to tell more than his name and address.
   In the face of his silence, the proper course to be followed by the interviewer is to

   A. remind the detainee that he is guilty of obstruction of justice
   B. stop the interrogation
   C. remind the detainee that his unwillingness to cooperate will result in high bail
   D. tell the interviewee he is required to cooperate with the police

4. *The implication in most discussions on police discretion is that it is the police administra-*   4.___
   tor who should undertake to spell out policies and rules.
   In the above statement, the word *discretion* means MOST NEARLY

   A. the power to judge or act
   B. behavior
   C. competence
   D. ability to reach a conclusion

5. A nickname for amphetamine is   5.___

   A. ice   B. pot   C. downer   D. grass

6. A nickname for cocaine is   6.___

   A. speed   B. red devils
   C. snow   D. Mary Jane

7. A nickname for marijuana is   7.___

   A. ice   B. downer   C. snow   D. grass

8. A nickname for barbiturates is   8.___

   A. angel dust   B. quaaludes
   C. meth   D. downers

9. Of the following, the most widely used drug is   9.____

   A. LSD   B. crack   C. marijuana   D. cocaine

10. Crack is related to   10.____

   A. angel dust   B. quaaludes
   C. LSD   D. cocaine

11. The police department is changing the type of ammunition they use. The new bullets will   11.____
    have a softer head. The main reason for this change is that

   A. it will not ricochet if it hits a wall
   B. it will cause less injury to a person struck by the bullet
   C. the bullet is less expensive
   D. it will be easier to recover

12. Of the following weapons, the one that is of the semiautomatic type is the   12.____

   A. Colt revolver   B. 45
   C. AK-47   D. Springfield rifle

13. A *Saturday Night Special* is a   13.____

   A. semi-automatic gun   B. small, cheaply made weapon
   C. gun used for hunting   D. difficult gun to conceal

14. One inch is equal to _____ centimeters.   14.____

   A. 2.54   B. 2.64   C. 2.74   D. 2.84

15. A gun control bill was passed in Congress that was named after President Reagan's   15.____
    press secretary who was shot in an attack on the President. The name of the bill was the
    _____ bill.

   A. McClure   B. Brady
   C. Volkmer   D. Everett Koop

16. In New York City, if you are caught carrying a concealed gun for which you do not have a   16.____
    permit, you can be jailed for a maximum of _____ months.

   A. 3   B. 6   C. 9   D. 12

17. The Federal Firearm License Law is designed to ensure that individuals who obtain   17.____
    licenses have a legitimate reason for doing so and to deny guns to

   A. people who carry large amounts of money on their person
   B. people who have a criminal record
   C. senior citizens
   D. people under 22 years old

18. According to government studies, the number of guns in the United States is over   18.____
    _____ million.

   A. one hundred   B. one hundred and twenty
   C. one hundred and fifty   D. two hundred

19. According to statistics, when a woman is killed with a gun, it is LEAST likely to be by   19.____

47

A. her husband   B. a relative
C. a stranger   D. a friend

20. Federal law states that a person is prohibited from buying a gun who is under the age of   20.__

     A. sixteen   B. eighteen
     C. twenty   D. twenty-two

21. Of the following countries in South America, the one that is the largest exporter of drugs   21.__
into the United States is

     A. Columbia   B. Venezuela
     C. Chile   D. Argentina

22. Of the following, the state in the United States that allows citizens to carry concealed   22.__
guns is

     A. Arizona   B. New Mexico
     C. Texas   D. Oklahoma

23. A bullet has a diameter of 9 mm. Its diameter, in inches, is MOST NEARLY _____ inch.   23.__

     A. 1/4   B. 3/8   C. 1/2   D. 5/8

24. The repeal of the amendment to the Constitution barring the manufacture and selling of   24.__
whiskey occurred under the administration of President

     A. Roosevelt   B. Hoover   C. Truman   D. Coolidge

25. The shrub from which cocaine is derived is   25.__

     A. cacao   B. hemp   C. liana   D. coca

KEY (CORRECT ANSWERS)

1. D		11. A	
2. D		12. C	
3. B		13. B	
4. A		14. A	
5. A		15. B	
6. C		16. D	
7. D		17. B	
8. D		18. D	
9. C		19. C	
10. D		20. B	

21. A
22. C
23. B
24. A
25. D

EXAMINATION SECTION
TEST 1

DIRECTIONS: Each question or incomplete statement is followed by several suggested answers or completions. Select the one that BEST answers the question or completes the statement. *PRINT THE LETTER OF THE CORRECT ANSWER IN THE SPACE AT THE RIGHT.*

1. When fighting fires in passenger airplanes, firemen usually attempt to rescue passengers and crew before putting out the flame. To accomplish the rescue, it is usually BEST to approach the burning airplane from the side   1._____

    A. where the fire is hottest
    B. where the generators are located
    C. where the reserve gas tanks are located
    D. which is nearest the fire apparatus
    E. where the doors are located

2. As soon as the engine pulled up to the scene of the fire, a fireman, axe in hand, jumped off, ran to the door, and broke it in. The action of this fireman was   2._____

    A. *wise;* he prepared the way for the hose men to move in
    B. *unwise;* he should have broken a window
    C. *wise;* speed is important in the rescue of fire victims
    D. *unwise;* he should have tried the door first to see if it was unlocked
    E. *unwise;* he should have first tried to locate the owner

3. Firefighters generally try to confine a fire to its point of origin. Of the following, the MOST important result of so doing is that   3._____

    A. property damage is minimized
    B. shorter hose lines are required
    C. immediate risks to fire forces are reduced
    D. fewer firemen are needed on the firefighting forces
    E. damage to fire equipment is reduced

4. Suppose you, a newly assigned fireman, are shown how to do a certain task by your lieutenant. You start the job but as you progress you encounter many difficulties. Of the following, the MOST desirable step for you to take at this time is to   4._____

    A. ask your lieutenant to suggest an easier way of doing the job
    B. speak to your lieutenant about your difficulties
    C. continue the task as well as you can
    D. stop what you are doing and do something else
    E. ask one of the older members for instructions

5. The one of the following statements about electric fuses that is MOST valid is that they   5._____

    A. should never be replaced by coins
    B. may be replaced by coins for a short time if there are no fuses available
    C. may be replaced by coins provided that the electric company is notified
    D. may be replaced by coins provided that care is taken to avoid overloading the circuit
    E. may be replaced only by a licensed electrician

6. A principal of an elementary school made a practice of holding fire drills on the last Friday of each month, just before normal dismissal. In general, conducting fire drills according to a regular schedule is

    A. *good;* pupils are more cooperative when fire drills result in early dismissal
    B. *bad;* fire drills should not be expected
    C. *good;* panic is avoided if the pupils know that there isn't a fire
    D. *bad;* holding fire drills once or twice a term is sufficient
    E. *good;* teachers can plan to finish their lessons before the fire drill

6.＿

7. It has been observed that persons in a burning building generally attempt to escape through the means provided for normal entry and exit. Of the following, the MOST likely reason for this is that

    A. people generally feel safer in groups
    B. people usually don't know the location of fire exits
    C. emergency exits are not easily reached
    D. the use of emergency exits requires physical dexterity
    E. people tend to behave in accordance with their habits

7.＿

8. A fireman inspecting a small retail store for hazardous fire conditions is told by the owner that the whole inspection procedure is a waste of time and money. Of the following, the BEST action for the fireman to take is to

    A. question the owner to prove to him how little he knows about the problem
    B. explain to the owner the benefits of the inspection program
    C. curtly tell the owner that he is entitled to his opinions and continue the inspection
    D. ask the owner if he can suggest a better way of preventing fires
    E. continue the inspection without answering the owner

8.＿

9. The officer in charge of operations at a fire has the responsibility for *sizing up* or evaluating the fire situation. Of the following factors, the one which would have LEAST influence on the *size up* is the

    A. time of fire
    B. contents of the building on fire
    C. insurance coverage
    D. amount of smoke
    E. height of the building on fire

9.＿

10. When searching burning houses, firemen usually pay particular attention to closets and the space under beds and furniture. Of the following, the MOST important reason for this practice is that often

    A. information about the cause of the fire may be found there
    B. children try to hide from danger in those places
    C. dogs and cats are forgotten in the excitement
    D. people mistake closet doors for exits
    E. valuable possessions may be found there

10.＿

11. When fighting fires, it is MOST important for a fireman to realize that in the winter

    11.____

    A. the water supply is more plentiful
    B. cold water is more effective than warm water in putting out fires
    C. snow conditions may delay fire apparatus
    D. water in hose lines not in use may freeze
    E. many fires are caused by heating equipment

12. Suppose you are a fireman making an inspection of a factory. During the inspection, the factory manager asks you a technical question which you cannot answer. Of the following, the BEST procedure for you to follow is to

    12.____

    A. tell him you are not there to answer his questions but to make an inspection
    B. guess at the answer so he won't doubt your competence
    C. tell him you don't know the answer but that you will look it up and notify him
    D. give him the title of a textbook that probably would contain the information
    E. change the subject by asking him a question

13. While performing building inspections, a fireman finds a janitor in the basement checking for a gas leak by holding a lighted match to the gas pipes. Of the following, the fireman's FIRST action should be to

    13.____

    A. reprimand the janitor for endangering life and property
    B. explain the hazards of this action to the janitor
    C. report the janitor to his superior as incompetent
    D. tell the janitor to put out the match
    E. issue a summons for this action

14. A fireman has complained to his lieutenant about drafts from loosely fitting windows in the bunk area of the firehouse. Several weeks pass and the condition has not been corrected. Of the following, the MOST appropriate action for the fireman to take at this time is to

    14.____

    A. ask the captain if the lieutenant has reported his complaint
    B. ask his lieutenant how the matter is coming along
    C. circulate a petition among the other members of the company to have this condition corrected
    D. write to the office of the Chief of the Department about the matter
    E. write to the Uniformed Firemen's Association about the matter

15. In answering an alarm, it is found that the fire has been caused by *smoking in bed,* setting fire to the mattress. The man is safe but the mattress is blazing. After putting out the flames, the mattress should be

    15.____

    A. turned over and left on the bed
    B. immediately ripped open and the stuffing examined
    C. taken into the bathroom and soaked in the tub
    D. taken to the street below and the stuffing examined
    E. thoroughly soaked in place by means of a hose stream

16. As a probationary fireman, you get an idea for improving equipment maintenance and mention it to an older member. At the next company inspection, your superior officer publicly praises this man for his excellent suggestion, but it is your idea. The action you should take in this situation is to

    A. tell the other members of the company the whole story after the inspection
    B. ask for advice from another older member
    C. forget about the incident since this man will probably be helpful to you in return
    D. do nothing about it but next time make your suggestions to your superior officer
    E. warn the older man that you won't permit him to get away with stealing your idea

16.__

17. The first rule of hosemen is to place themselves in the line of travel of a fire whenever possible. Of the following, the MOST valid reason for this rule is that

    A. danger to firemen from heat and smoke is reduced
    B. shorter hose lines are necessary
    C. the opportunity to control the fire is increased
    D. danger to fire equipment is reduced
    E. life-saving rescues are facilitated

17.__

18. Of the following types of fires, the one which presents the GREATEST danger from poisonous gas fumes is a fire in a warehouse storing

    A. drugs   B. groceries
    C. cotton cloth   D. paper
    E. unfinished furniture

18.__

19. Fires in prisons and mental hospitals are particularly dangerous to life CHIEFLY because their inmates usually

    A. live under crowded conditions
    B. live in locked rooms
    C. ignore fire safety regulations
    D. deliberately start fires
    E. cannot be trusted with fire extinguishers

19.__

20. In fighting fires, use the smallest amount of water sufficient to put out the fire. In general, this advice is

    A. *good,* mainly because it will conserve the water supply
    B. *bad,* mainly because it will increase the danger of the fire spreading
    C. *good,* mainly because it will require the use of fewer hose lines
    D. *bad,* mainly because it will take longer to put out the fire
    E. *good,* mainly because it will reduce water damage

20.__

21. The Fire Department has criticized the management of several hotels for failure to call the Fire Department promptly when fires are discovered. The MOST probable reason for this delay by the management is that

    A. fire insurance rates are affected by the number of fires reported
    B. most fires are extinguished by the hotels' staff before the Fire Department arrives
    C. hotel guests frequently report fires erroneously
    D. it is feared that hotel guests will be alarmed by the arrival of fire apparatus
    E. many fires smolder for a long time before they are discovered

21.__

22. A fireman, taking some clothing to a dry cleaner in his neighborhood, noticed that inflammable cleaning fluid was stored in a way which created a fire hazard. The fireman called this to the attention of the proprietor, explaining the danger involved. This method of handling the situation was

    22._____

    A. *bad;* the fireman should not have interfered in a matter which was not his responsibility
    B. *good;* the proprietor would probably remove the hazard and be more careful in the future
    C. *bad;* the fireman should have reported the situation to the fire inspector's office without saying anything to the proprietor
    D. *good;* since the fireman was a customer, he should treat the proprietor more leniently than he would treat other violators
    E. *bad;* the fireman should have ordered the proprietor to remove the violation immediately and issued a summons

23. Traditionally, firemen have attacked fires with solid streams of water from hose lines. A new development in firefighting is to break up the solid water stream as it leaves the hose nozzle into a large number of tiny droplets, called a fog stream. Of the following claimed advantages of a solid stream, as compared to a fog stream, the one that is MOST valid is that a solid stream

    23._____

    A. has greater cooling effect per gallon of water
    B. causes less water damage
    C. results in less drain on the water supply
    D. involves less risk of walls collapsing
    E. can be used at a greater distance from the fire

24. A fireman caught a civilian attempting to re-enter a burning building despite several warnings to stay outside of the fire lines. The civilian insisted frantically that he must save some very valuable documents from the fire. The fireman then called a policeman to remove the civilian. The fireman's action was

    24._____

    A. *wrong;* it is bad public relations to order people about
    B. *right;* the fireman is charged with the responsibility of protecting lives
    C. *wrong;* the fireman should have explained to the civilian why he should not enter the building
    D. *right;* civilians must be excluded from the fire zone
    E. *wrong;* every person has a right to risk his own life as he sees fit

25. A lieutenant orders a fireman to open the windows in a room filled with smoke. He starts with the window nearest the entrance and follows the wall around the room until all the windows are opened. The MOST important reason for using this procedure is that he can

    25._____

    A. avoid stumbling over furniture
    B. breathe the fresher air near the walls
    C. locate unconscious persons at the same time
    D. avoid the weakened floor in the middle of the room
    E. find his way back to the entrance

26. One purpose of building inspections is to enable the Fire Department to plan its operations before a fire starts.
This statement is

    A. *incorrect;* no two fires are alike
    B. *correct;* many firefighting problems can be anticipated
    C. *incorrect;* fires should be prevented, not extinguished
    D. *correct;* the fire Department should have detailed plans for every possible emergency
    E. *incorrect;* fires are not predictable 3

26.__

27. A recent study showed that false alarms occur mostly between Noon and 1 P.M., and between 3 and 10 P.M.
The MOST likely explanation of these results is many false alarms are sent by

    A. school children   B. drunks
    C. mental defectives   D. arsonists
    E. accident victims

27.__

28. A superintendent of a large apartment house discovered a fire in a vacant apartment. After notifying the Fire Department, he went to the basement and shut off the central air conditioning system. In so doing, the superintendent acted

    A. *wisely;* escape of gas fumes from the air conditioning system was prevented
    B. *unwisely;* the fire would have been slowed down by the cooling effect of the air conditioning
    C. *wisely;* the air conditioning system was protected from damage by the fire
    D. *unwisely;* the air conditioning system would have expelled smoke from the building
    E. *widely;* spread of the fire by means of a forced draft was prevented

28.__

29. Large woolen blankets are unsatisfactory as emergency life nets CHIEFLY because they usually are

    A. too small to catch a falling person
    B. difficult to grasp since they have no handles
    C. difficult to maneuver into position
    D. not circular in shape as are regular life nets
    E. not tensile enough to hold falling bodies

29.__

30. Fires can be fought most effectively from close range. Of the following, the CHIEF obstacle preventing firemen from getting close to fires is the

    A. heat of the fire
    B. height of most city buildings
    C. distance from the hydrants of most fires
    D. inaccessible location of most fires
    E. wide area covered by the fire

30.__

31. While in training school, your class assists at a fire. After the fire is under control, an older fireman, who has no authority over you, tells you that he was watching you perform your tasks. He suggests certain changes in your methods. Of the following, your BEST course of action is to

31.__

A. thank him for his advice and tell him you will use it when you find yourself in diffi-culty
B. discuss the changes he proposed with him and then take the action which seems best to you
C. listen to his analysis of the situation and follow his advice
D. thank him for his advice and bring up his suggestions at the next class session
E. listen to him, thank him courteously, but ignore his suggestions

32. A member of a fire rescue company discovers an injured man at the foot of the stairway on the third floor of a burning building. The man, who fell down the stairs, complains of pains in his back. The fire is a considerable distance away, in the cellar, but the area is rapidly filling with smoke. Of the following, the BEST course for the fireman to follow is to   32.____

A. give the injured man first aid on the spot and leave him there
B. carefully carry the injured man to safety
C. stay with the injured man to make certain that the fire doesn't reach him
D. find his officer and ask for instructions
E. go for medical assistance

33. Listed below are five operating characteristics of most automatic sprinkler systems. The one characteristic of those listed which is LEAST desirable is that automatic sprinkler systems   33.____

A. operate only in the fire zone
B. go into operation soon after a fire starts
C. operate in the midst of high heat and smoke
D. continue operating after the fire is extinguished
E. operate in inaccessible places

34. The extinguisher must be inverted before it will operate. As used in this sentence, the word inverted means MOST NEARLY   34.____

A. turned over
B. completely filled
C. lightly shaken
D. unhooked
E. opened

35. Sprinkler systems in buildings can retard the spread of fires. As used in this sentence, the word retard means MOST NEARLY   35.____

A. quench
B. outline
C. slow
D. reveal
E. aggravate

36. Although there was widespread criticism, the director refused to curtail the program. As used in this sentence, the word curtail means MOST NEARLY   36.____

A. change
B. discuss
C. shorten
D. expand
E. enforce

37. Argon is an inert gas. As used in this sentence, the word inert means MOST NEARLY   37.____

A. unstable
B. uncommon
C. volatile
D. inferior
E. inactive

38. The firemen turned their hoses on the shed and the main building <u>simultaneously.</u> As used in this sentence, the word <u>simultaneously</u> means MOST NEARLY

    A. in turn   B. without hesitation
    C. with great haste   D. as needed
    E. at the same time

38.__

39. The officer was <u>rebuked</u> for his failure to act promptly. As used in this sentence, the word <u>rebuked</u> means MOST NEARLY

    A. demoted   B. reprimanded   C. discharged
    D. reassigned   E. suspended

39.__

40. Parkways in the city may be used to <u>facilitate</u> responses to alarms. As used in this sentence, the word <u>facilitate</u> means MOST NEARLY

    A. reduce   B. alter   C. complete
    D. ease   E. control

40.__

41. Fire extinguishers are most effective when the fire is <u>incipient.</u> As used in this sentence, the word <u>incipient</u> means MOST NEARLY

    A. accessible   B. beginning   C. red hot
    D. confined   E. smoky

41.__

42. It is important to <u>convey to</u> new members the fundamental methods of firefighting. As used in this sentence, the words <u>convey to</u> means MOST NEARLY

    A. inquire   B. prove for   C. confirm for
    D. suggest to   E. impart to

42.__

43. The explosion was a <u>graphic</u> illustration of the effects of neglect and carelessness. As used in this sentence, the word <u>graphic</u> means MOST NEARLY

    A. terrible   B. poor   C. typical
    D. unique   E. vivid

43.__

44. The fireman was <u>assiduous</u> in all things relating to his duties. As used in this sentence, the word <u>assiduous</u> means MOST NEARLY

    A. aggressive   B. careless   C. persistent
    D. cautious   E. dogmatic

44.__

45. A fireman must be <u>adept</u> to be successful at his work.
As used in this sentence, the word <u>adept</u> means MOST NEARLY

    A. ambitious   B. strong   C. agile
    D. alert   E. skillful

45.__

46. Officers shall see that parts are issued in <u>consecutive</u> order. As used in this sentence, the word <u>consecutive</u> means MOST NEARLY

    A. objective   B. random   C. conducive
    D. effective   E. successive

46.__

47. Practically every municipality has fire ordinances. As used in this sentence, the word ordinances means MOST NEARLY   47.____

    A. drills   B. stations   C. engines
    D. laws   E. problems

48. When the smoke cleared away, the fireman's task was alleviated. As used in this sentence, the word alleviated means MOST NEARLY   48.____

    A. lessened   B. visible   C. appreciated
    D. safer   E. accomplished

49. The conflagration spread throughout the entire city. As used in this sentence, the word conflagration means MOST NEARLY   49.____

    A. hostilities   B. confusion   C. rumor
    D. epidemic   E. fire

50. The fireman purged the gas tank after emptying its contents. As used in this sentence, the word purged means MOST NEARLY   50.____

    A. sealed   B. punctured   C. exposed
    D. cleansed   E. buried

KEY (CORRECT ANSWERS)

1.	E	11.	D	21.	D	31.	D	41.	B
2.	D	12.	C	22.	B	32.	B	42.	E
3.	A	13.	D	23.	E	33.	D	43.	E
4.	B	14.	B	24.	B	34.	A	44.	C
5.	A	15.	D	25.	E	35.	C	45.	E
6.	B	16.	D	26.	B	36.	C	46.	E
7.	E	17.	C	27.	A	37.	E	47.	D
8.	B	18.	A	28.	E	38.	E	48.	A
9.	C	19.	B	29.	E	39.	B	49.	E
10.	B	20.	E	30.	A	40.	D	50.	D

TEST 2

DIRECTIONS: Each question or incomplete statement is followed by several suggested answers or completions. Select the one that BEST answers the question or completes the statement. *PRINT THE LETTER OF THE CORRECT ANSWER IN THE SPACE AT THE RIGHT.*

1. Spontaneous combustion may be the reason for a pile of oily rags catching fire. In general, spontaneous combustion is the direct result of   1.__

    A. application of flame   B. falling sparks
    C. intense sunlight   D. chemical action
    E. radioactivity

2. In general, firemen are advised not to direct a solid stream of water on fires burning in electrical equipment. Of the following, the MOST logical reason for this instruction is that   2.__

    A. water is a conductor of electricity
    B. water will do more damage to the electrical equipment than the fire
    C. hydrogen in water may explode when it comes in contact with electric current
    D. water will not effectively extinguish fires in electrical equipment
    E. water may spread the fire to other circuits

3. The height at which a fireboat will float in still water is determined CHIEFLY by the   3.__

    A. weight of the water displaced by the boat
    B. horsepower of the boat's engine
    C. number of propellers on the boat
    D. curve the bow has above the water line
    E. skill with which the boat is maneuvered

4. When firemen are working at the nozzle of a hose, they usually lean forward on the hose. The MOST likely reason for taking this position is that   4.__

    A. the surrounding air is cooled, making the firemen more comfortable
    B. a backward force is developed which must be counteracted
    C. the firemen can better see where the stream strikes
    D. the firemen are better protected from injury by falling debris
    E. the stream is projected further

5. In general, the color and odor of smoke will BEST indicate   5.__

    A. the cause of the fire
    B. the extent of the fire
    C. how long the fire has been burning
    D. the kind of material on fire
    E. the exact seat of the fire

6. As a demonstration, firemen set up two hose lines identical in every respect except that one was longer than the other. Water was then delivered through these lines from one pump and it was seen that the stream from the longer hose line had a shorter *throw*. Of the following, the MOST valid explanation of this difference in *throw* is that the   6.__

    A. air resistance to the water stream is proportional to the length of hose
    B. time required for water to travel through the longer hose is greater than for the shorter one

C. loss due to friction is greater in the longer hose than in the shorter one
D. rise of temperature is greater in the longer hose than in the shorter one
E. longer hose line probably developed a leak at one of the coupling joints

7. Of the following toxic gases, the one which is MOST dangerous because it cannot be seen and has no odor is   7.____

   A. ether   B. carbon monoxide
   C. chlorine   D. ammonia
   E. cooking gas

8. You are visiting with some friends when their young son rushes into the room with his clothes on fire. You immediately wrap him in a rug and roll him on the floor. The MOST important reason for your action is that the   8.____

   A. flames are confined within the rug
   B. air supply to the fire is reduced
   C. burns sustained will be third degree, rather than first degree
   D. whirling action will put out the fire
   E. boy will not suffer from shock

9. A fireman discovers a man bleeding moderately from a gash wound about 1 1/2" long in his right arm. Of the following, the FIRST action this fireman should take is to   9.____

   A. apply a tourniquet between the wound and the heart
   B. permit the bleeding to continue for a while in order to cleanse the wound
   C. give the injured man a blood transfusion
   D. apply pressure at the nearest pressure point between the wound and the heart
   E. apply pressure directly to the wound with compress

10. In treating burns, the LEAST important of the following goals is to   10.____

   A. prevent blistering   B. prevent infection
   C. relieve pain   D. prevent shock
   E. prevent tissue damage

11. The Battalion District in Manhattan is bounded on the north by Fifth Avenue, the west by the Hudson River, the south by 30th Street, and the east by Madison Avenue. The above statement is WRONG in that   11.____

   A. none of the boundary lines intersect
   B. Fifth Avenue cannot be a northern boundary
   C. the Hudson River cannot be a western boundary
   D. 30th Street cannot be a southern boundary
   E. Madison Avenue cannot be an eastern boundary

12. Of the following, the MAIN reason the Police Department is using some unmarked or unidentified patrol cars is to   12.____

   A. catch car thieves red-handed
   B. observe patrolmen in the performance of their duty
   C. reduce the expense of police equipment
   D. trap juvenile gangs
   E. reduce the number of traffic accidents

Questions 13-16.

DIRECTIONS: Questions 13 through 16, inclusive, are based on the following paragraph.

Ventilation, as used in firefighting operations, means opening up a building or structure in which a fire is burning to release the accumulated heat, smoke, and gases. Lack of knowledge of the principles of ventilation on the part of firemen may result in unnecessary punishment due to ventilation being neglected or improperly handled. While ventilation itself extinguishes no fires, when used in an intelligent manner, it allows firemen to get at the fire more quickly, easily, and with less danger and hardship.

13. According to the above paragraph, the MOST important result of failure to apply the principles of ventilation at a fire may be   13

    A. loss of public confidence
    B. disciplinary action
    C. waste of water
    D. excessive use of equipment
    E. injury to firemen

14. It may be inferred from the above paragraph that the CHIEF advantage of ventilation is that it   14

    A. eliminates the need for gas masks
    B. reduces smoke damage
    C. permits firemen to work closer to the fire
    D. cools the fire
    E. enables firemen to use shorter hose lines

15. Knowledge of the principles of ventilation, as defined in the above paragraph, would be LEAST important in a fire in a   15

    A. tenement house   B. grocery store
    C. ship's hold   D. lumberyard
    E. office building

16. We may conclude from the above paragraph that for the well-trained and equipped firemen, ventilation is   16

    A. a simple matter   B. rarely necessary
    C. relatively unimportant   D. a basic tool
    E. sometimes a handicap

Questions 17-19.

DIRECTIONS: Questions 17 through 19 are based on the following paragraph.

A fire of undetermined origin started in the warehouse shed of a flour mill. Although there was some delay in notifying the fire department, they practically succeeded in bringing the fire under control when a series of dust explosions occurred which caused the fire to spread and the main building was destroyed. The fire department's efforts were considerably handicapped because it was undermanned, and the water pressure in the vicinity was inadequate.

17. From the information contained in the above paragraph, it is MOST accurate to state that the cause of the fire was   17.____

    A. suspicious   B. unknown
    C. accidental   D. arson
    E. spontaneous combustion

18. In the fire described above, the MOST important cause of the fire spreading to the main building was the   18.____

    A. series of dust explosions
    B. delay in notifying the fire department
    C. inadequate water pressure
    D. lack of manpower
    E. wooden construction of the building

19. In the fire described above, the fire department's efforts were handicapped CHIEFLY by   19.____

    A. poor leadership
    B. outdated apparatus
    C. uncooperative company employees
    D. insufficient water pressure
    E. poorly trained men

Questions 20-22.

DIRECTIONS: Questions 20 through 22, inclusive, are based on the following paragraph.

A flameproof fabric is defined as one which, when exposed to small sources of ignition such as sparks or smoldering cigarettes, does not burn beyond the vicinity of the source of the ignition. Cotton fabrics are the materials commonly used that are considered most hazardous. Other materials, such as acetate rayons and linens, are somewhat less hazardous, and woolens and some natural silk fabrics, even when untreated, are about the equal of the average treated cotton fabric insofar as flame spread and ease of ignition are concerned. The method of application is to immerse the fabric in a flameproofing solution. The container used must be large enough so that all the fabric is thoroughly wet and there are no folds which the solution does not penetrate.

20. According to the above paragraph, a flameproof fabric is one which   20.____

    A. is unaffected by heat and smoke
    B. resists the spread of flames when ignited
    C. burns with a cold flame
    D. cannot be ignited by sparks or cigarettes
    E. may smolder but cannot burn

21. According to the above paragraph, woolen fabrics which have not been flameproofed are as likely to catch fire as _____ fabrics.   21.____

    A. treated silk   B. treated acetate rayon
    C. untreated linen   D. untreated synthetic
    E. treated cotton

22. In the method described above, the flameproofing solution is BEST applied to the fabric   22.
by _____ the fabric.

   A. sponging   B. spraying   C. dipping
   D. brushing   E. sprinkling

Questions 23-26.

DIRECTIONS: Questions 23 through 26, inclusive, are based on the following paragraph.

There is hardly a city in the country that is not short of fire protection in some areas
within its boundaries. These municipalities have spread out and have re-shuffled their resi-
dential, business, and industrial districts without readjusting the existing protective fire forces,
or creating new protection units. Fire stations are still situated according to the needs of earlier times and have not been altered or improved to house modern firefighting equipment.
They are neither efficient for carrying out their tasks nor livable for the men who must occupy
them.

23. Of the following, the title which BEST describes the central idea of the above paragraph   23.
is THE

   A. DYNAMIC NATURE OF CONTEMPORARY SOCIETY
   B. COST OF FIRE PROTECTION
   C. LOCATION AND DESIGN OF FIRE STATIONS
   D. DESIGN AND USE OF FIREFIGHTING EQUIPMENT
   E. GROWTH OF AMERICAN CITIES

24. According to the above paragraph, fire protection is inadequate in the United States in   24.
_____ areas _____ cities.

   A. most; of some   B. some; of most
   C. some; in all   D. all; in some
   E. most; in most

25. The one of the following criteria for planning of fire stations which is NOT mentioned in   25.
the above paragraph is

   A. comfort of firemen
   B. proper location
   C. design for modern equipment
   D. efficiency of operation
   E. cost of construction

26. Of the following suggestions for improving the fire service, the one which would BEST   26.
deal with the problem discussed in the paragraph above would involve

   A. specialized training in the use of modern fire apparatus
   B. replacement of obsolete fire apparatus
   C. revision of zoning laws
   D. longer basic training for probationary firemen
   E. reassignment of fire districts

Questions 27-29.

DIRECTIONS: The sentences listed below are part of a meaningful paragraph, but they are
not given in their proper order. You are to decide what would be the BEST
order in which to put the sentences so as to form a well-organized paragraph.
Each sentence has a place in the paragraph; there are no extra sentences.
You are then to answer Questions 27 through 29, inclusive, on the basis of
your rearrangement of these scrambled sentences into a properly organized
paragraph. It will help you in answering the questions to jot down the correct
order of the sentences in the margins.

In 1887, some insurance companies organized an Inspection Department to advise their
clients on all phases of fire prevention and protection. Probably this has been due to the
smaller annual fire losses in Great Britain than in the United States. It tests various fire prevention devices and appliances and determines manufacturing hazards and their safeguards.
Fire research began earlier in the United States and is more advanced than in Great Britain.
Later, they established a laboratory specializing in electrical, mechanical, hydraulic, and
chemical fields.

27.   When the five sentences above are arranged in proper order, the paragraph starts with   27._____
the sentence which begins

A.   In 1887   B.   Probably this
C.   It tests   D.   Fire research
E.   Later they

28.   In the last sentence listed above, *they* refers to   28._____

A.   insurance companies
B.   the United States and Great Britain
C.   the Inspection Department
D.   clients
E.   technicians

29.   When the above paragraph is properly arranged, it ends with the words   29._____

A.   . . . protection   B.   . . . the United States
C.   . . . their safeguards   D.   . . . in Great Britain
E.   . . . chemical fields

Questions 30-32.

DIRECTIONS: Questions 30 through 32, inclusive, are to be answered with reference to the
device shown below.

The device shown in Figure 1 represents schematically a mechanism commonly used to
change reciprocating (back and forth) motion to rotating (circular) motion.

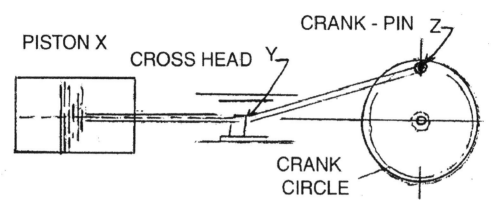

FIGURE 1

30. Assume that piston X is placed in its extreme left position so that X, Y, and Z are in a hor- 30.__
    izontal line. If a horizontal force to the right is applied to the piston X, we may then expect
    that

    A. the crank-pin Z will revolve clockwise
    B. the crosshead Y will move in a direction opposite to that of X
    C. the crank-pin Z will revolve counterclockwise
    D. no movement will take place
    E. the crank-pin Z will oscillate back and forth

31. If we start from the position shown in the diagram above and move piston X to the right,   31.__
    the result will be that

    A. the crank-pin Z will revolve counterclockwise and crosshead Y will move to the left
    B. the crank-pin Z will revolve clockwise and crosshead Y will move to the left
    C. the crank-pin Z will revolve counterclockwise and crosshead Y will move to the
        right
    D. the crank-pin Z will revolve clockwise and crosshead Y will move to the right
    E. crosshead Y will move to the left as piston X moves to the right

32. If crank-pin Z is moved closer to the center of the crank circle, then the length of the   32.__

    A. stroke of piston X is increased
    B. stroke of piston X is decreased
    C. stroke of piston X is unchanged
    D. rod between the piston X and crosshead Y is increased
    E. rod between the piston X and crosshead Y is decreased

Questions 33-34.

DIRECTIONS: Figure II represents schematically a block and fall tackle. The advantage
             derived from this machine is that the effect of the applied force is multiplied by
             the number of lines of rope directly supporting the load. Questions 33 and 34
             are to be answered with reference to this figure.

33. Pull P is exerted on Line T to raise the load L. The line in which the LARGEST strain is finally induced is line

33.____

A. T
B. U
C. V
D. X
E. Y.

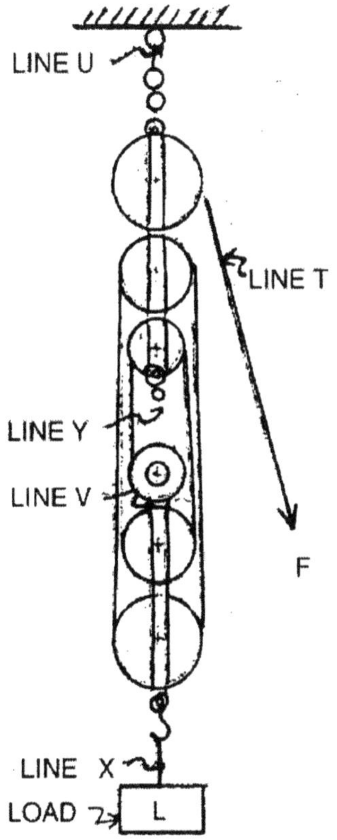

34. If the largest Pull P that two men can apply to Line T is 280 lbs., the MAXIMUM load L that they can raise without regard to frictional losses is MOST NEARLY _____ lbs.

34.____

A. 1960
B. 1680
C. 1400
D. 1260
E. 1120

FIGURE II

35. Rules must be applied with discretion.
As used in this sentence, the word discretion means MOST NEARLY

35.____

A. impartiality   B. judgment   C. severity
D. patience   E. consistency

36. The officer and his men ascended the stairs as rapidly as they could.
As used in this sentence, the word ascended means MOST NEARLY

36.____

A. went up   B. washed down   C. chopped
D. shored up   E. inspected

37. The store's refusal to accept delivery of the merchandise was a violation of the express provisions of the contract. As used in this sentence, the word express means MOST NEARLY

37.____

A. clear   B. implied   C. penalty
D. disputed   E. complicated

38. A fire engine carries 900 feet of 2 1/2 hose, 500 feet of 2" hose, and 350 feet of 1 1/2 hose. Of the total hose carried, the percentage of 1 1/2 hose is MOST NEARLY

38.____

A. 35   B. 30   C. 25   D. 20   E. 15

39. An engine company made 96 runs in the month of April which was a decrease of 20% from the number of runs made in March. The number of runs made in March was MOST NEARLY

39.____

A. 136   B. 128   C. 120   D. 110   E. 112

65

40. A water tank has a capacity of 6000 gallons. Connected to the tank is a pump capable of   40.__
supplying water at the rate of 25 gallons per minute which goes into operation automatically when the water in the tank falls to the one-half mark. If we start with a full tank and
drain the water from the tank at the rate of 50 gallons a minute, the tank can continue
supplying water at the required rate for _____ hours.

    A. 2 1/2   B. 3   C. 3 1/2   D. 4   E. 4 1/2

41. Three firemen are assigned the task of cleaning fire apparatus which usually takes three   41.__
men five hours to complete. After they have been working three hours, three additional
firemen are assigned to help them. Assuming that they all work at the normal rate, the
assignment of the additional men will reduce the time required to complete the task by
_____ minutes.

    A. 20   B. 30   C. 40   D. 50   E. 60

42. Assume that at the beginning of the calendar year an employee was earning $4,800 per   42.__
year. On July 1st, he received an increase of $240 per year. On November 1st, he was
promoted to a position paying $6,000 per year. The total earnings for the year were
MOST NEARLY

    A. $5,100   B. $4,900   C. $5,000   D. $5,400   E. $5,300

43. Engine A leaves its firehouse at 1:48 P.M. and travels 3 miles to a fire at an average   43.__
speed of 30 miles per hour. Engine B leaves its firehouse at 1:51 P.M. and travels 6 miles
to the same fire at an average speed of 40 miles per hour. From the above facts, we may
conclude that Engine A arrives _____ Engine B.

    A. 3 minutes before   B. 6 minutes before
    C. 3 minutes after   D. 6 minutes after
    E.   at the same time as

44. A widely used formula for calculating the quantity of water discharged from a hose is: 44.__

    $GPM = 29.7d^2 \sqrt{P}$, where GPM = gallons per minute, d = diameter of the nozzle in
inches, and P = pressure at the nozzle in pounds per square inch. If it takes 1 minute to
extinguish a fire using a 1 1/2" nozzle at 100 pounds pressure per square inch, the number of gallons discharged is, according to the above formula, MOST NEARLY

    A. 730   B. 650   C. 710   D. 690   E. 670

45. The spring of a spring balance will stretch in proportion to the amount of weight placed   45.__
on the balance. If a 2-pound weight placed on a certain balance stretches the spring 1/4"
then a stretch in the spring of 1 3/4" will be caused by a weight of _____ pounds.

    A. 10   B. 12   C. 14   D. 16

KEY (CORRECT ANSWERS)

1.	D	11.	B	21.	E	31.	D	41.	E
2.	A	12.	E	22.	C	32.	B	42.	A
3.	A	13.	E	23.	C	33.	B	43.	B
4.	B	14.	C	24.	B	34.	B	44.	E
5.	D	15.	D	25.	E	35.	B	45.	C
6.	C	16.	D	26.	E	36.	A		
7.	B	17.	B	27.	D	37.	A		
8.	B	18.	A	28.	A	38.	D		
9.	E	19.	D	29.	C	39.	C		
10.	A	20.	B	30.	D	40.	B		

EXAMINATION SECTION
TEST 1

DIRECTIONS: Each question or incomplete statement is followed by several suggested answers or completions. Select the one that BEST answers the question or completes the statement. *PRINT THE LETTER OF THE CORRECT ANSWER IN THE SPACE AT THE RIGHT.*

1. According to the American Red Cross, the proper IMMEDIATE first aid care for a frost-bitten hand is to   1.____

    A. rub the hand with snow
    B. place the part in warm water
    C. cover the hand with a woolen cloth
    D. vigorously rub the hands together

2. The symptoms of heat exhaustion are   2.____

    A. pale, clammy skin, low temperature, weak pulse
    B. rapid and strong pulse, dry skin, high temperature
    C. headache, red face, unconsciousness
    D. abdominal cramps, red skin, profuse sweating

3. Arterial pressure points   3.____

    A. are best located by taking the pulse
    B. lie close to bones near the surface of the body
    C. are used to cut off all blood circulation
    D. are deepseated and require great pressure

4. Of the following, the one NOT recommended for the first aid of burns is   4.____

    A. boric acid   B. baking soda
    C. petrolatum ointment   D. Epsom salts

5. A person who has fainted should be   5.____

    A. propped up on a pillow or head rest
    B. given a warm drink
    C. aroused as soon as possible
    D. laid flat and kept quiet

6. Of the following associations of symptom(s) and sudden illness or accident, the INCORRECT one is   6.____

    A. blood spurting from the wrist - cut artery
    B. stoppage of breathing - suffocation
    C. pale, cold, moist skin - shock
    D. partial tearing of ligaments of a joint - strain

7. In the care of a sprained ankle, an INCORRECT procedure in first aid would be to   7.____

    A. elevate the sprained part   B. apply cold applications
    C. massage the part to restore circulation   D. apply a temporary support

8. In administering first aid, one should encourage bleeding by mild pressure, being careful   8._
    not to bruise the tissue, in wounds classified as

     A.   punctures   B.   incisions   C.   lacerations   D.   abrasions

9. All of the following first aid rules for simple nosebleeds may be safely followed EXCEPT   9._

     A.   gently pinching the nostrils together
     B.   applying cold compresses to the nose
     C.   blowing the nose gently after bleeding stops to remove blood clots
     D.   inserting a plug of absorbent cotton in each of the nostrils

10. Of the following associations of symptom and illness, the one which is INCORRECT is   10._

     A.   cough - onset of measles
     B.   pallor - anemia
     C.   sore throat - impetigo
     D.   red eyes, accompanied by a discharge - conjunctivitis

———

KEY (CORRECT ANSWERS)

1.	C		6.	D
2.	A		7.	C
3.	B		8.	A
4.	A		9.	C
5.	D		10.	C

———

TEST 2

DIRECTIONS: Each question or incomplete statement is followed by several suggested answers or completions. Select the one that BEST answers the question or completes the statement. *PRINT THE LETTER OF THE CORRECT ANSWER IN THE SPACE AT THE RIGHT.*

1. The MAJORITY of home accidents result from

    A. burns   B. suffocation   C. falls   D. poisons

1.____

2. Of the following, the one that is NOT a symptom of shock is

    A. flushed face   B. weak pulse
    C. cold, clammy skin   D. feeling of weakness

2.____

3. The purpose of applying artificial respiration to the victim of an electric shock is to

    A. restore blood circulation
    B. avoid excessive loss of blood
    C. keep the victim warm
    D. supply oxygen to the lungs

3.____

4. The INCORRECT procedure in treating nosebleeds is to

    A. have the victim lie down immediately
    B. apply a large cold, wet cloth to the nose
    C. pack the nose gently with gauze
    D. press the nostrils firmly together

4.____

5. In one minute, the heart of a normal man who is resting beats APPROXIMATELY _____ times.

    A. 30   B. 72   C. 98   D. 112

5.____

6. In attempting to revive a person who has stopped breathing after receiving an electric shock, it is MOST important to

    A. start artificial respiration immediately
    B. wrap the victim in a blanket
    C. massage the ankles and wrists
    D. force the victim to swallow a stimulant

6.____

7. In the Holger-Nielsen method of artificial respiration, the victim is placed

    A. on his stomach   B. on his back
    C. in a kneeling position   D. in any comfortable position

7.____

8. Frequent deaths are reported as a result of running an automobile engine in a closed garage.
Death results from

    A. suffocation
    B. carbon monoxide poisoning
    C. excessive humidity
    D. an excess of carbon dioxide in the air

8.____

9. Fever, chills, inflamed eyelids, running nose, and cough are symptoms of   9.__

    A. measles   B. chicken pox
    C. tuberculosis   D. scarlet fever

10. Among the usual signs of measles are listlessness, red watery eyes that are sensitive to   10.__
light, a moderate fever, and

    A. a running nose   B. a blotchy red rash
    C. a running ear   D. convulsions

———————

KEY (CORRECT ANSWERS)

1.	C		6.	A
2.	A		7.	A
3.	D		8.	B
4.	A		9.	A
5.	B		10.	A

———————

TEST 3

1. To provide transit employees with quick assistance in the case of minor injuries, it would be MOST logical to   1.____

    A. instruct the employees in first aid techniques
    B. provide each employee with a first aid kit
    C. have one centrally located medical office for the transit system
    D. equip all employees with walkie-talkie devices

2. If a person has just received an electric shock and appears dead, the FIRST two things that a rescuer should do in proper order are: 2.____

    A. Wrap the victim in a blanket and free him from the circuit
    B. Free the victim from the circuit and wrap him in a blanket
    C. Free the victim from the circuit and give him a stimulant
    D. Free the victim from the circuit and apply artificial respiration

3. In the back pressure, arm-lift method of artificial respiration, each full cycle should be administered steadily at a rate per minute of   3.____

    A. 12 to 15 times   B. 70 to 80 times
    C. 20 to 30 times   D. once

4. During an epileptic seizure, the patient should be   4.____

    A. given a drink of water or stimulant
    B. held securely so that he will not struggle
    C. carried to the medical office immediately
    D. left where he has fallen and prevented from injuring himself

5. When a person suffers a compound fracture of the leg, in all probability the damaged bone is the   5.____

    A. radius or ulna   B. clavicle
    C. sternum   D. tibia or fibula

6. The overall purpose of the application of heat to a victim in shock is to   6.____

    A. cause sweating
    B. prevent a large loss of body heat
    C. increase the body's temperature
    D. increase the blood circulation

7. The American Red Cross recommends that an abrasion be treated by   7.____

    A. applying iodine
    B. covering the wound with gauze
    C. washing the wound with soap and water
    D. applying mercurochrome

8. Of the following, the symptom of heatstroke MOST frequently noted is   8.__

    A. an absence of perspiration
    B. mental confusion
    C. headache
    D. dilated pupils

9. A puncture wound is considered serious from the point of view that   9.__

    A. bleeding may be hard to stop
    B. injury to tissue may be extensive
    C. infection is likely to result
    D. multiple injury may result

10. The method of resuscitation MOST generally accepted today is the _____ method.   10.__

    A. back pressure arm lift   B. mouth to mouth
    C. Sylvester   D. Schaefer

KEY (CORRECT ANSWERS)

1.	A		6.	B
2.	D		7.	C
3.	A		8.	A
4.	D		9.	C
5.	D		10.	B

TEST 4

DIRECTIONS: Each question or incomplete statement is followed by several suggested answers or completions. Select the one that BEST answers the question or completes the statement. *PRINT THE LETTER OF THE CORRECT ANSWER IN THE SPACE AT THE RIGHT.*

1. Suppose that, as a uniformed officer, you are called to administer first aid to an unconscious person.
   Of the following, the BEST reason for NOT attempting to administer a liquid stimulant to this person is that

   A. he may have poor circulation of blood
   B. he may choke on the liquid
   C. stimulants affect the heart
   D. stimulants should be administered at the direction of a physician

   1.____

2. Assume that it is necessary for you to apply a tourniquet in order to stop serious bleeding.
   The one of the following MOST properly used for this purpose is

   A. thin cord   B. thick rope   C. a necktie   D. wire

   2.____

3. Suppose that an elderly man has met with an accident and is lying on the floor awaiting the arrival of a doctor. Of the following, the BEST action to take in order to prevent shock is to

   A. raise him to a sitting position
   B. apply a wet cloth to his head
   C. apply artificial respiration
   D. cover him with a coat

   3.____

4. While you are on duty, a fellow officer suddenly turns pale and his breathing becomes rapid and shallow. He is apparently suffering from heat exhaustion.
   Of the following, the LEAST desirable action for you to take under the circumstances is to

   A. apply cold cloths to his head
   B. place him in a reclining position
   C. give him a stimulant
   D. have him sip salt water

   4.____

5. Assume that a fellow officer is in contact with an electrically charged wire.
   Of the following, the BEST reason for NOT grasping the victim's clothing with your bare hands in order to pull him off the wire is that

   A. his clothing may be damp with perspiration
   B. his clothing may be 100% wool
   C. you may be standing on a dry surface
   D. you may be wearing rubber-soled shoes

   5.____

6. Suppose a man falls from a two-story high scaffold and is unconscious. You should

    A. call for medical assistance and avoid moving the man
    B. get someone to help you move him indoors to a bed
    C. have someone help you walk him around until he revives
    D. hold his head up and pour a stimulant down his throat

6._

7. For proper first aid treatment, a person who has fainted should be

    A. doused with cold water and then warmly covered
    B. given artificial respiration until he is revived
    C. laid down with his head lower than the rest of his body
    D. slapped on the face until he is revived

7._

8. If you are called on to give first aid to a person who is suffering from shock, you should

    A. apply cold towels   B. give him a stimulant
    C. keep him awake   D. wrap him warmly

8._

9. Artificial respiration would NOT be proper first aid for a person suffering from

    A. drowning   B. electric shock
    C. external bleeding   D. suffocation

9._

10. Suppose you are called on to give first aid to several victims of an accident. First attention should be given to the one who is

    A. bleeding severely   B. groaning loudly
    C. unconscious   D. vomiting

10._

KEY (CORRECT ANSWERS)

1.	B	6.	A
2.	C	7.	C
3.	D	8.	D
4.	A	9.	C
5.	A	10.	A

TEST 5

DIRECTIONS: Each question or incomplete statement is followed by several suggested answers or completions. Select the one that BEST answers the question or completes the statement. *PRINT THE LETTER OF THE CORRECT ANSWER IN THE SPACE AT THE RIGHT.*

1. Suppose that, while you are on patrol, a teenage boy dashes out of a dry cleaning store, his clothes afire.
   The BEST action for you to take in this situation is to

   1.____

   A. stop the boy and roll him in a coat to smother the flames
   B. lead the boy quickly to the nearest store and douse him with large quantities of water
   C. remove all burning articles of clothing from the boy as quickly as possible
   D. take the boy back into the dry cleaning store where a fire extinguisher will almost certainly be available to extinguish the flames quickly

2. A woman comes running towards you crying that her child was bitten by their pet dog.
   The FIRST action you should take is to

   2.____

   A. summon a doctor so that he may treat the wounds
   B. shoot the dog to prevent it from biting others
   C. have the child put to bed
   D. apply ice packs to the wounds until the pain subsides

3. You are called to an apartment house to stop a quarrel between a husband and wife. When you arrive there, you find that the husband has left and that the woman is lying unconscious on the floor. In the meantime, a neighbor has telephoned for an ambulance.

   You note that the room temperature is about 50°.
   The FIRST action is to

   3.____

   A. rub the hands of the woman to keep her blood circulating
   B. make her drink hot tea or coffee to try to revive her
   C. place a hot water bottle under her feet to keep them warm
   D. place one blanket underneath her and another one over her

4. As a person who is well-informed in the fundamentals of giving first aid, you should know that the *Schaefer Method* is MOST helpful for

   4.____

   A. stopping bleeding
   B. transporting injured persons
   C. promoting respiration
   D. stopping the spread of infection

5. While you are on duty, a middle-aged man crossing the street cries out with pain, presses his hands to his chest, and stands perfectly still. You suspect that he may have suffered a heart attack.
   You should

   5.____

   A. ask him to cross the street quickly in order to prevent his being hit by moving traffic
   B. permit him to lie down flat in the street while you divert the traffic

C. ask him for the name of his doctor so that you can summon him
D. request a cab to take him to the nearest hospital for immediate treatment

6. When administering first aid for the accidental swallowing of poison, water is given CHIEFLY to   6.__

   A. increase energy   B. quiet the nerves
   C. weaken the poison   D. prevent choking

7. The CHIEF purpose of administering artificial respiration to first aid is to   7.__

   A. exert regular pressure on the heart
   B. force the blood into circulation by pressure
   C. force air into the lungs
   D. keep the person warm by keeping his body in motion

8. When severe shock occurs, it is important for the person being treated to have   8.__

   A. sedatives and cold drinks
   B. warmth and low head position
   C. hot drinks and much activity
   D. sedatives and sitting position

9. When administering first aid, a tourniquet is used to   9.__

   A. sterilize the injured area
   B. hold the splits in place
   C. hold the dressing in place
   D. stop the loss of blood

10. Heat exhaustion and sunstroke are alike in that in both cases the person affected   10.__

    A. has hot dry skin and a red face
    B. should lie with head high
    C. should be given stimulants
    D. has been exposed to heat

KEY (CORRECT ANSWERS)

1.	A	6.	C
2.	A	7.	C
3.	D	8.	B
4.	C	9.	D
5.	B	10.	D

READING COMPREHENSION
UNDERSTANDING AND INTERPRETING WRITTEN MATERIAL
EXAMINATION SECTION
TEST 1

DIRECTIONS: Each question has five suggested answers, lettered A to E. Decide which one
is the BEST answer. *PRINT THE LETTER OF THE CORRECT ANSWER IN
THE SPACE AT THE RIGHT.*

1. Some specialists are willing to give their services to the Government entirely free of   1.____
charge; some feel that a nominal salary, such as will cover traveling expenses, is sufficient for a position that is recognized as being somewhat honorary in nature; many other
specialists value their time so highly that they will not devote any of it to public service
that does not repay them at a rate commensurate with the fees that they can obtain from
a good private clientele.
*The paragraph BEST supports the statement that the use of specialists by the Govern-
ment*

   A.   is rare because of the high cost of securing such persons
   B.   may be influenced by the willingness of specialists to serve
   C.   enables them to secure higher salaries in private fields
   D.   has become increasingly common during the past few years
   E.   always conflicts with private demands for their services

2. The fact must not be overlooked that only about one-half of the international trade of the   2.____
world crosses the oceans. The other half is merely exchanges of merchandise between
countries lying alongside each other or at least within the same continent.
The paragraph BEST supports the statement that

   A.   the most important part of any country's trade is transoceanic
   B.   domestic trade is insignificant when compared with foreign trade
   C.   the exchange of goods between neighborhing countries is not considerd interna-
tional trade
   D.   foreign commerce is not necessarily carried on by water
   E.   about one-half of the trade of the world is international

3. Individual differences in mental traits assume importance in fitting workers to jobs   3.____
because such personal characteristics are persistent and are relatively little influenced
by training and experience.
The paragraph BEST supports the statement that training and experience

   A.   are limited in their effectiveness in fitting workers to jobs
   B.   do not increase a worker's fitness for a job
   C.   have no effect upon a person's mental traits
   D.   have relatively little effect upon the individual's chances for success
   E.   should be based on the mental traits of an individual

4. The competition of buyers tends to keep prices up, the competition of sellers to send   4.__
   them down. Normally the pressure of competition among sellers is stronger than that
   among buyers since the seller has his article to sell and must get rid of it, whereas the
   buyer is not committed to anything.
   The paragraph BEST supports the statement that low prices are caused by

   A. buyer competition
   B. competition of buyers with sellers
   C. fluctuations in demand
   D. greater competition among sellers than among buyers
   E. more sellers than buyers

5. In seventeen states, every lawyer is automatically a member of the American Bar Associ-   5.__
   ation. In some other states and localities, truly representative organizations of the Bar
   have not yet come into being, but are greatly needed.
   The paragraph IMPLIES that

   A. representative Bar Associations are necessary in states where they do not now
      exist
   B. every lawyer is required by law to become a member of the Bar
   C. the Bar Association is a democratic organization
   D. some states have more lawyers than others
   E. every member of the American Bar Association is automatically a lawyer in seven-
      teen states.

   _____

KEY (CORRECT ANSWERS)

1. B
2. D
3. A
4. D
5. A

   _____

TEST 2

DIRECTIONS: Each question has five suggested answers, lettered A to E. Decide which one is the BEST answer. *PRINT THE LETTER OF THE CORRECT ANSWER IN THE SPACE AT THE RIGHT.*

1. We hear a great deal about the new education, and see a great deal of it in action. But the school house, though prodigiously magnified in scale, is still very much the same old school house.
    The paragraph IMPLIES that
    1._____

    A. the old education was, after all, better than the new
    B. although the modern school buildings are larger than the old ones, they have not changed very much in other respects
    C. the old school houses do not fit in with modern educational theories
    D. a fine school building does not make up for poor teachers
    E. schools will be schools

2. No two human beings are of the same pattern — not even twins and the method of bringing out the best in each one necessarily varies according to the nature of the child.
    The paragraph IMPLIES that
    2._____

    A. individual differences should be considered in dealing with children
    B. twins should be treated impartially
    C. it is an easy matter to determine the special abilities of children
    D. a child's nature varies from year to year
    E. we must discover the general technique of dealing with children

3. Man inhabits today a world very different from that which encompassed even his parents and grandparents. It is a world geared to modern machinery—automobiles, airplanes, power plants; it is linked together and served by electricity.
    The paragraph IMPLIES that
    3._____

    A. the world has not changed much during the last few generations
    B. modern inventions and discoveries have brought about many changes in man's way of living
    C. the world is run more efficiently today than it was in our grandparents' time
    D. man is much happier today than he was a hundred years ago
    E. we must learn to see man as he truly is, underneath the veneers of man's contrivances

4. Success in any study depends largely upon the interest taken in that particular subject by the student. This being the case, each teacher earnestly hopes that her students will realize at the very outset that shorthand can be made an intensely fascinating study.
    The paragraph IMPLIES that
    4._____

    A. everyone is interested in shorthand
    B. success in a study is entirely impossible unless the student finds the study very interesting
    C. if a student is eager to study shorthand, he is likely to succeed in it
    D. shorthand is necessary for success
    E. anyone who is not interested in shorthand will not succeed in business

5. The primary purpose of all business English is to move the reader to agreeable and mutually profitable action. This action may be indirect or direct, but in either case a highly competitive appeal for business should be clothed with incisive diction tending to replace vagueness and doubt with clarity, confidence, and appropriate action.
   The paragraph IMPLIES that the

5.__

   A. ideal business letter uses words to conform to the reader's language level
   B. business correspondent should strive for conciseness in letter writing
   C. keen competition of today has lessened the value of the letter as an appeal for business
   D. writer of a business letter should employ incisive diction to move the reader to compliant and gainful action
   E. the writer of a business letter should be himself clear, confident, and Forceful

---

KEY (CORRECT ANSWERS)

1. B
2. A
3. B
4. C
5. D

TEST 3

DIRECTIONS: Each question has five suggested answers, lettered A to E. Decide which one is the BEST answer. *PRINT THE LETTER OF THE CORRECT ANSWER IN THE SPACE AT THE RIGHT.*

1. To serve the community best, a comprehensive city plan must coordinate all physical improvements, even at the possible expense of subordinating individual desires, to the end that a city may grow in a more orderly way and provide adequate facilities for its people.
   The paragraph IMPLIES that

   A. city planning provides adequate facilities for recreation
   B. a comprehensive city plan provides the means for a city to grow in a more orderly fashion
   C. individual desires must always be subordinated to civic changes
   D. the only way to serve a community is to adopt a comprehensive city plan
   E. city planning is the most important function of city government

   1.____

2. Facility in writing letters, the knack of putting into these quickly written letters the same personal impression that would mark an interview, and the ability to boil down to a one-page letter the gist of what might be called a five- or ten-minute conversation—all these are essential to effective work under conditions of modern business organization.
   The paragraph IMPLIES that

   A. letters are of more importance in modern business activities than ever before
   B. letters should be used in place of interviews
   C. the ability to write good letters is essential to effective work in modern business organization
   D. business letters should never be more than one page in length
   E. the person who can write a letter with great skill will get ahead more readily than others

   2.____

3. The general rule is that it is the city council which determines the amount to be raised by taxation and which therefore determines, within the law, the tax rates. As has been pointed out, however, no city council or city authority has the power to determine what kinds of taxes should be levied.
   The paragraph IMPLIES that

   A. the city council has more authority than any other municipal body
   B. while the city council has a great deal of authority in the levying of taxes, its power is not absolute
   C. the kinds of taxes levied in different cities vary greatly
   D. the city council appoints the tax collectors
   E. the mayor determines the kinds of taxes to be levied

   3.____

4. The growth of modern business has made necessary mass production, mass distribution, and mass selling. As a result, the problems of personnel and industrial relations have increased so rapidly that grave injustices in the handling of personal relationships have frequently occurred. Personnel administration is complex because, as in all human problems, many intangible elements are involved. Therefore a thorough, systematic, and continuous study of the psychology of human behavior is essential to the intelligent handling of personnel.
   The paragraph IMPLIES that

   4.____

A. complex modern industry makes impossible the personal relationships which formerly existed between employer and employee
B. mass decisions are successfully applied to personnel problems
C. the human element in personnel administration makes continuous study necessary to its intelligent application
D. personnel problems are less important than the problems of mass production and mass distribution
E. since personnel administration is so complex and costly, it should be subordinated to the needs of good industrial relations

5. The Social Security Act is striving toward the attainment of economic security for the individual and for his family. It was stated, in outlining this program, that security for the individual and for the family concerns itself with three factors: (1) decent homes to live in; (2) development of the natural resources of the country so as to afford the fullest opportunity to engage in productive work; and (3) safeguards against the major misfortunes of life. The Social Security Act is concerned with the third of these factors – "safeguards against misfortunes which cannot be wholly eliminated in this man-made world of ours."
   The paragraph IMPLIES that the

   A. Social Security Act is concerned primarily with supplying to families decent homes in which to live
   B. development of natural resources is the only means of offering employment to the
   C. masses of the unemployed
      Social Security Act has attained absolute economic security for the individual and his family
   D. Social Security Act deals with the first (1) factor as stated in the paragraph above
   E. Social Security Act deals with the third (3) factor as stated in the paragraph above

_____

KEY (CORRECT ANSWERS)

1. B
2. C
3. B
4. C
5. E

_____

TEST 4

Free unrhymed verse has been practiced for some thousands of years and reaches back to the incantation which linked verse with the ritual dance. It provided a communal emotion; the aim of the cadenced phrases was to create a state of mind. The general coloring of free rhythms in the poetry of today is that of speech rhythm, composed in the sequence of the musical phrase, not in the sequence of the metronome, the regular beat. In the twenties, conventional rhyme fell into almost complete disuse. This liberation from rhyme became as well a liberation of rhyme. Freed of its exacting task of supporting lame verse, it would be applied with greater effect where wanted for some special effect. Such break in the tradition of rhymed verse had the healthy effect of giving it a fresh start, released from the hampering convention of too familiar cadences. This refreshing and subtilizing of the use of rhyme can be seen everywhere in the poetry today.

1. The title below that BEST expresses the ideas of this paragraph is: 1.____

    A. Primitive Poetry
    B. The Origin of Poetry
    C. Rhyme and Rhythm in Modern Verse
    D. Classification of Poetry
    E. Purposes in All Poetry

2. Free verse had its origin in primitive   2.____

    A. fairytales   B. literature   C. warfare
    D. chants   E. courtship

3. The object of early free verse was to   3.____

    A. influence the mood of the people   B. convey ideas
    C. produce mental pictures   D. create pleasing sounds
    E. provide enjoyment

PASSAGE 2

Control of the Mississippi had always been goals of nations having ambitions in the New World. La Salle claimed it for France in 1682. Iberville appropriated it to France when he colonized Louisiana in 1700. Bienville founded New Orleans, its principal port, as a French city in 1718. The fleur-de-lis were the blazon of the delta country until 1762. Then Spain claimed all of Louisiana. The Spanish were easy neighbors. American products from western Pennsylvania and the North west Territory were barged down the Ohio and Mississippi to New Orleans, here they were reloaded on ocean-going vessels that cleared for the great seaports of the world.

1. The title below that BEST expresses the ideas of this paragraph is: 1.____

    A. Importance of seaports
    B. France and Spain in the New World
    C. Early control of the Mississippi
    D. Claims of European nations
    E. American trade on the Mississippi

2. Until 1762 the lower Mississippi area was held by

    A. England   B. Spain   C. the United States
    D. France   E. Indians

2.

3. In doing business with Americans the Spaniards were

    A. easy to outsmart
    B. friendly to trade
    C. inclined to charge high prices for use of their ports
    D. shrewd
    E. suspicious

3.

PASSAGE 3

Our humanity is by no means so materialistic as foolish talk is continually asserting it to be. Judging by what I have learned about men and women, I am convinced that there is far more in them of idealistic willpower than ever comes to the surface of the world. Just as the water of streams is small in amount compared to that which flows underground, so the idealism which becomes visible is small in amount compared with that which men and women bear locked in their hearts, unreleased or scarcely released. To unbind what is bound, to bring the underground waters to the surface — mankind is waiting and longing for men who can do that.

1. The title below that BEST expresses the ideas of this paragraph is

    A. Releasing Underground Riches
    B. The Good and Bad in Man
    C. Materialism in Humanity
    D. The Surface and the Depths of Idealism
    E. Unreleased Energy

1.

2. Human beings are more idealistic than

    A. the water in underground streams
    B. their waiting and longing proves
    C. outward evidence shows
    D. the world
    E. other living creatures

2.

PASSAGE 4

The total impression made by any work of fiction cannot be rightly understood without a sympathetic perception of the artistic aims of the writer. Consciously or unconsciouly, he has accepted certain facts, and rejected or suppressed other facts, in order to give unity to the particular aspect of human life which he is depicting. No novelist possesses the impartiality, the indifference, the infinite tolerance of nature. Nature displays to use, with complete unconcern, the beautiful and the ugly, the precious and the trivial, the pure and the impure. But a writer must select the aspects of nature and human nature which are demanded by the work in hand. He is forced to select, to combine, to create.

1. The title below that BEST expresses the ideas of this paragraph is: 1.____

    A. Impressionists in Literature
    B. Nature as an Artist
    C. The Novelist as an Imitator
    D. Creative Technic of the Novelist
    E. Aspects of Nature

2. A novelist rejects some facts because they   2.____

    A. are impure and ugly
    B. would show he is not impartial
    C. are unrelated to human nature
    D. would make a bad impression
    E. mar the unity of his story

3. It is important for a reader to know   3.____

    A. the purpose of the author
    B. what facts the author omits
    C. both the ugly and the beautiful
    D. something about nature
    E. what the author thinks of human nature

PASSAGE 5

If you watch a lamp which is turned very rapidly on and off, and you keep your eyes open, "persistence of vision" will bridge the gaps of darkness between the flashes of light, and the lamp will seem to be continuously lit. This "topical afterglow" explains the magic produced by the stroboscope, a new instrument which seems to freeze the swiftest motions while they are still going on, and to stop time itself dead in its tracks. The "magic" is all in the eye of the beholder.

1. The "magic" of the stroboscope is due to   1.____

    A. continuous lighting   B. intense cold
    C. slow motion   D. behavior of the human eye
    E. a lapse of time

2. "Persistence of vision" is explained by   2.____

    A. darkness   B. winking   C. rapid flashes
    D. gaps   E. after impression

87

KEY (CORRECT ANSWERS)

PASSAGE 1

1. C
2. D
3. A

PASSAGE 2

1. C
2. D
3. B

PASSAGE 3

1. D
2. C

PASSAGE 4

1. D
2. E
3. A

PASSAGE 5

1. D
2. E

TEST 5

PASSAGE 1

During the past fourteen years, thousands of top-lofty United States elms have been marked for death by the activities of the tiny European elm bark beetle. The beetles, however, do not do fatal damage. Death is caused by another importation, Dutch elm disease, a fungus infection which the beetles carry from tree to tree. Up to 1941, quarantine and tree-sanitation measures kept the beetles and the disease pretty well confined within 510 miles around metropolitan New York. War curtailed these measures and made Dutch elm disease a wider menace. Every house hold and village that prizes an elm-shaded lawn or commons must now watch for it. Since there is as yet no cure for it, the infected trees must be pruned or felled, and the wood must be burned in order to protect other healthy trees.

1. The title below that BEST expresses the ideas of this paragraph is: 1.____

    A. A Menace to Our Elms   B. Pests and Diseases of the Elm
    C. Our Vanishing Elms   D. The Need to Protect Dutch Elms
    E. How Elms are Protected

2. The danger of spreading the Dutch elm disease was increased by   2.____

    A. destroying infected trees   B. the war
    C. the lack of a cure   D. a fungus infection
    E. quarantine measures

3. The European elm bark beetle is a serious threat to our elms because it   3.____

    A. chews the bark
    B. kills the trees
    C. is particularly active on the eastern seaboard
    D. carries infection
    E. cannot be controlled

PASSAGE 2

It is elemental that the greater the development of man, the greater the problems he has to concern him. When he lived in a cave with stone implements, his mind no less than his actions was grooved into simple channels. Every new invention, every new way of doing things posed fresh problems for him. And, as he moved along the road, he questioned each step, as indeed he should, for he trod upon the beliefs of his ancestors. It is equally elemental to say that each step upon this later road posed more questions than the earlier ones. It is only the edcated man who realizes the results of his actions; it is only the thoughtful one who questions his own decisions.

1. The title below that BEST expresses the ideas of this paragraph is: 1.____

    A. Channels of Civilization
    B. The Mark of a Thoughtful Man
    C. The Cave Man in Contrast with Man Today
    D. The Price of Early Progress
    E. Man's Never-Ending Challenge

PASSAGE 3

Spring is one of those things that man has no hand in, any more than he has a part in sunrise or the phases of the moon. Spring came before man was here to enjoy it, and it will go right on coming even if man isn't here some time in the future. It is a matter of solar mechanics and celestial order. And for all our knowledge of astronomy and terrestrial mechanics, we haven't yet been able to do more than bounce a radar beam off the moon. We couldn't alter the arrival of the spring equinox by as much as one second, if we tried.

Spring is a matter of growth, of chlorophyll, of bud and blossom. We can alter growth and change the time of blossoming in individual plants; but the forests still grow in nature's way, and the grass of the plains hasn't altered its nature in a thousand years. Spring is a magnificent phase of the cycle of nature; but man really hasn't any guiding or controlling hand in it. He is here to enjoy it and benefit by it. And April is a good time to realize it; by May perhaps we will want to take full credit.

1. The title below that BEST expresses the ideas of this passage is:

    A. The Marvels of the Spring Equinox
    B. Nature's Dependence on Mankind
    C. The Weakness of Man Opposed to Nature
    D. The Glories of the World
    E. Eternal Growth

2. The author of the passage states that

    A. man has a part in the phases of the moon
    B. April is a time for taking full-credit
    C. April is a good time to enjoy nature
    D. man has a guiding hand in spring
    E. spring will cease to be if civilization ends

PASSAGE 4

The walled medieval town was as characteristic of its period as the cut of a robber baron's beard. It sprang out of the exigencies of war, and it was not without its architectural charm, whatever its hygienic deficiencies may have been. Behind its high, thick walls not only the normal inhabitants but the whole countryside fought and cowered in an hour of need. The capitals of Europe now forsake the city when the sirens scream and death from the sky seems imminent. Will the fear of bombs accelerate the slow decentralization which began with the automobile and the wide distribution of electrical energy and thus reverse the medieval flow to the city?

1. The title below that BEST expresses the ideas in this paragraph is.

A. A Changing Function of the Town	B. The Walled Medieval Town
C. The Automobile's Influence on City Life	D. Forsaking the City
E. Bombs Today and Yesterday	

2. Conditions in the Middle Ages made the walled town

A. a natural development	B. the most dangerous of all places
C. a victim of fires	D. lacking in architectural charm
E. healthful	

3. Modern conditions may   3.____

    A. make cities larger   B. make cities more hygienic
    C. protect against floods   D. cause people to move from population
    E. encourage good architecture   centers

PASSAGE 5

The literary history of this nation began when the first settler from abroad of sensitive mind paused in his adventure long enough to feel that he was under a different sky, breathing new air, and that a New World was all before him with only his strength and Providence for guides. With him began a new emphasis upon an old theme in literature, the theme of cutting loose and faring forth, renewed, under the powerful influence of a fresh continent for civilized man. It has provided, ever since those first days, a strong current in our native literature, whose other flow has come from a nostalgia for the rich culture of Europe, so much of which was perforce left behind.

1. The title below that BEST expresses the ideas of this paragraph is: 1.____

    A. America's Distinctive Literature   B. Pioneer Authors
    C. The Dead Hand of the Past   D. Europe's Literary Grandchild
    E. America Comes of Age

2. American writers, according to the author, because of their colonial experiences   2.____

    A. were antagonistic to European writers
    B. cut loose from Old World influences
    C. wrote only on New World events and characters
    D. created new literary themes
    E. gave fresh interpretation to an old literary idea

KEY (CORRECT ANSWERS)

PASSAGE 1	PASSAGE 2
1. A	1. E
2. B	
3. D	

PASSAGE 3	PASSAGE 4
1. C	1. A
2. C	2. A
	3. D

PASSAGE 5

1. A
2. E

TEST 6

1. Any business not provided with capable substitutes to fill all important positions is a weak business. Therefore a foreman should train each man not only to perform his own particular duties but also to do those of two or three positions.
    The paragraph BEST supports the statement that

    A. dependence on substitutes is a sign of weak organization
    B. training will improve the strongest organization
    C. the foreman should be the most expert at any particular job under him
    D. every employee can be trained to perform efficiently work other than his own
    E. vacancies in vital positions should be provided for in advance

    1.___

2. The coloration of textile fabrics composed of cotton and wool generally requires two processes, as the process used in dyeing wool is seldom capable of fixing the color upon cotton. The usual method is to immerse the fabric in the requisite baths to dye the wool and then to treat the partially dyed material in the manner found suitable for cotton.
    The paragraph BEST supports the statement that the dyeing of textile fabrics composed of cotton and wool

    A. is less complicated than the dyeing of wool alone
    B. is more successful when the material contains more cotton than wool
    C. is not satisfactory when solid colors are desired
    D. is restricted to two colors for any one fabric
    E. is usually based upon the methods required for dyeing the different materials

    2.___

3. The serious investigator must direct his whole effort toward. success in his work. If he wishes to succeed in each investigation, his work will be by no means easy, smooth, or peaceful; on the contrary, he will have to devote himself completely and continuously to a task that requires all his ability.
    The paragraph BEST supports the statement that an investigator's success depends most upon

    A. ambition to advance rapidly in the service
    B. persistence in the face of difficulty
    C. training and experience
    D. willingness to obey orders without delay
    E. the number of investigations which he conducts

    3.___

4. Honest people in one nation find it difficult to understand the viewpoint of honest people in another. State departments and their ministers exist for the purpose of explaining the viewpoints of one nation in terms understood by another. Some of their most important work lies in this direction.
    The paragraph BEST supports the statement that

    A. people of different nations may not consider matters in the same light
    B. it is unusual for many people to share similar ideas
    C. suspicion prevents understanding between nations
    D. the chief work of state departments is to guide relations between nations united by a common cause
    E. the people of one nation must sympathize with the view points of others

    4.___

5. Economy once in a while is just not enough. I expect to find it at every level of responsi-   5.____
   bility, from cabinet member to the newest and youngest recruit. Controlling waste is
   something like bailing a boat; you have to keep at it. I have no intention of easing up on
   my insistence on getting a dollar of value for each dollar we spend.
   The paragraph BEST supports the statement that

   A. we need not be concerned about items which cost less than a dollar
   B. it is advisable to buy the cheaper of two items
   C. the responsibility of economy is greater at high levels than at low levels
   D. economy becomes easy with practice
   E. economy is a continuing responsibility

_____

KEY (CORRECT ANSWERS)

1. E
2. E
3. B
4. A
5. E

_____

TEST 7

1. On all permit imprint mail the charge for postage has been printed by the mailer before   1.___
   he presents it for mailing and pays the postage. Such mail of any class is mailable only at
   the post office that issued a permit covering it. Since the postage receipts for such mail
   represent only the amount of permit imprint mail detected and verified, employees in
   receiving, handling, and outgoing sections must be alert constantly to route such mail to
   the weighing section before it is handled or dispatched.
   The paragraph BEST supports the statement that, at post offices where permit mail is
   received for dispatch,

   A. dispatching units make a final check on the amount of postage payable on permit
      imprint mail
   B. employees are to check the postage chargeable on mail received under permit
   C. neither more nor less postage is to be collected than the amount printed on permit
      imprint mail
   D. the weighing section is primarily responsible for failure to collect postage on such
      mail
   E. unusual measures are taken to prevent unstamped mail from being accepted

2. Education should not stop when the individual has been prepared to make a livelihood   2.___
   and to live in modern society. Living would be mere existence were there no appreciation
   and enjoyment of the riches of art, literature, and science.
   The paragraph BEST supports the statement that true education

   A. is focused on the routine problems of life
   B. prepares one for full enjoyment of life
   C. deals chiefly with art, literature and science
   D. is not possible for one who does not enjoy scientific literature
   E. disregards practical ends

3. Insured and c.o.d. air and surface mail is accepted with the understanding that the   3.___
   sender guarantees any necessary forwarding or return postage. When such mail is forwarded or returned, it shall be rated up for collection of postage; except that insured or
   c.o.d. air mail weighing 8 ounces or less and subject to the 40 cents an ounce rate shall
   be forwarded by air if delivery will be advanced, and returned by surface means, without
   additional postage.
   The paragraph BEST supports the statement that the return postage for undeliverable
   insured mail is

   A. included in the original prepayment on air mail parcels
   B. computed but not collected before dispatching surface patrol post mail to sender
   C. not computed or charged for any air mail that is returned by surface transportation
   D. included in the amount collected when the sender mails parcel post
   E. collected before dispatching for return if any amount due has been guaranteed

4. All undeliverable first-class mail, except first-class parcels and parcel post paid with first-   4.___
   class postage, which cannot be returned to the sender, is sent to a dead-letter branch.
   Undeliverable matter of the third-and fourth-classes of obvious value for which the
   sender does not furnish return postage and undeliverable first-class parcels and parcel-
   post matter bearing postage of the first-class, which cannot be returned, is sent to a
   dead parcel-post branch.

The paragraph BEST supports the statement that matter that is sent to a dead parcel-post branch includes all undeliverable

- A. mail, except first-class letter mail, that appears to be valuable
- B. mail, except that of the first-class, on which the sender failed to prepay the original mailing costs
- C. parcels on which the mailer prepaid the first-class rate of postage
- D. third-and fourth-class matter on which the required return postage has not been paid
- E. parcels on which first-class postage has been prepaid, when the sender's address is not known

5. Civilization started to move rapidly when man freed himself of the shackles that restricted his search for truth.
   The paragraph BEST supports the statement that the progress of civilization

   5.____

- A. came as a result of man's dislike for obstacles
- B. did not begin until restrictions on learning were removed
- C. has been aided by man's efforts to find the truth
- D. is based on continually increasing efforts
- E. continues at a constantly increasing rate

———

KEY (CORRECT ANSWERS)

1. B
2. B
3. B
4. E
5. C

———

TEST 8

1. E-mails should be clear, concise, and brief. Omit all unnecessary words. The parts of speech most often used in e-mails are nouns, verbs, adjectives, and adverbs. If possible, do without pronouns, prepositions, articles, and copulative verbs. Use simple sentences, rather than complex and compound.
   The paragraph BEST supports the statement that in writing e-mails one should always use

   A. common and simple words
   B. only nouns, verbs, adjectives, and adverbs
   C. incomplete sentences
   D. only words essential to the meaning
   E. the present tense of verbs

1.__

2. The function of business is to increase the wealth of the country and the value and happiness of life. It does this by supplying the material needs of men and women. When the nation's business is successfully carried on, it renders public service of the highest value.
   The paragraph BEST supports the statement that

   A. all businesses which render public service are successful
   B. human happiness is enhanced only by the increase of material wants
   C. the value of life is increased only by the increase of wealth
   D. the material needs of men and women are supplied by welt-conducted business
   E. business is the only field of activity which increases happiness

2.__

3. In almost every community, fortunately, there are certain men and women known to be public-spirited. Others, however, may be selfish and act only as their private interests seem to require.
   The paragraph BEST supports the statement that those citizens who disregard others are

   A. fortunate   B. needed
   C. found only in small communities   D. not known
   E. not public-spirited

3.__

KEY (CORRECT ANSWERS)

1. D
2. D
3. E

READING COMPREHENSION
UNDERSTANDING AND INTERPRETING WRITTEN MATERIAL

EXAMINATION SECTION
TEST 1

DIRECTIONS: Each question or incomplete statement is followed by several suggested answers or completions. Select the one that BEST answers the question or completes the statement. *PRINT THE LETTER OF THE CORRECT ANSWER IN THE SPACE AT THE RIGHT.*

Questions 1-4.

DIRECTIONS: Questions 1 through 4 are to be answered SOLELY on the basis of the following paragraph.

The canister-type gas mask consists of a tight-fitting face piece connected to a canister containing chemicals which filter toxic gases and smoke from otherwise breathable air. These masks are of value when used with due regard to the fact that two or three percent of gas in air is about the highest concentration that the chemicals in the canister will absorb and that these masks do not provide the oxygen which is necessary for the support of life. In general, if flame is visible, there is sufficient oxygen for firefighters although toxic gases may be present. Where there is heavy smoke and no flame, an oxygen deficiency may exist. Fatalities have occurred where filter-type canister masks have been used in attempting rescue from manholes, wells, basements, or other locations deficient in oxygen.

1. If the mask described above is used in an atmosphere containing oxygen, nitrogen, and carbon monoxide, we would expect the mask to remove from the air breathed   1.____

    A.   the nitrogen only
    B.   the carbon monoxide only
    C.   the nitrogen and the carbon monoxide
    D.   none of these gases

2. According to the above paragraph, when a fireman is wearing one of these masks at a fire where flame is visible, he can GENERALLY feel that as far as breathing is concerned, he is   2.____

    A.   *safe*, since the mask will provide him with sufficient oxygen to live
    B.   *unsafe*, unless the gas concentration is below 2 or 3 percent
    C.   *safe*, provided the gas concentration is above 2 or 3 percent
    D.   *unsafe*, since the mask will not provide him with sufficient oxygen to live

3. According to the above paragraph, fatalities have occurred to persons using this type gas mask in manholes, wells, and basements because   3.____

    A.   the supply of oxygen provided by the mask ran out
    B.   the air in those places did not contain enough oxygen to support life
    C.   heavy smoke interfered with the operation of the mask
    D.   the chemicals in the canister did not function properly

4. The following shorthand formula may be used to show, in general, the operation of the gas mask described in the above paragraph:
(Chemicals in canister) → (Air + gases) = Breathable Air.
The arrow in the formula, when expressed in words, means MOST NEARLY

   A. replace
   C. act upon
                           B. are changed into
                           D. give off

4.

Questions 5-7.

DIRECTIONS: Questions 5 through 7 are to be answered SOLELY on the basis of the following paragraph.

The only openings permitted in fire partitions, except openings for ventilating ducts, shall be those required for doors. There shall be but one such door opening unless the provision of additional openings would not exceed in total width of all doorways 25 percent of the length of the wall. The minimum distance between openings shall be three feet. The maximum area for such a door opening shall be 80 square feet, except that such openings for the passage of motor trucks may be a maximum of 140 square feet.

5. According to the above paragraph, openings in fire partitions are permitted ONLY for

   A. doors
   B. doors and windows
   C. doors and ventilation ducts
   D. doors, windows, and ventilation ducts

5.

6. In a fire partition 22 feet long and 10 feet high, the MAXIMUM number of doors 3 feet wide and 7 feet high is

   A. 1   B. 2   C. 3   D. 4

6.

7.

7.

The one of the following statements about the layout shown above that is MOST accurate is that the

A. total width of the openings is too large
B. truck opening is too large
C. truck and door openings are too close together
D. layout is acceptable

Questions 8-11.

DIRECTIONS: Questions 8 through 11 are to be answered SOLELY on the basis of the following paragraph.

Division commanders shall arrange and maintain a plan for the use of hose wagons to
transport members in emergencies. Upon receipt of a call for members, the deputy chief of
the division from whom the men are called shall have the designated hose wagon placed out
of service and prepared for the transportation of members. Hose wagons shall be placed at
central assembly points, and members detailed instructed to report promptly to such locations equipped for fire duty. Hose wagons designated shall remain at regular assignments
when not engaged in the transportation of members.

8. Preparation of the hose wagon for this special assignment of transporting of members   8.____
   would MOST likely involve

   A. checking the gas and oil, air in tires, and mechanical operation of the apparatus
   B. removal of hose lines to make room for the members being transported
   C. gathering of equipment which will be needed by the members being transported
   D. instructing the driver on the best route to be used

9. Hose wagons used for emergency transportation of members are placed out of service   9.____
   because they are

   A. not available to respond to alarms in their own district
   B. more subject to mechanical breakdown while on emergency duty
   C. engaged in operations which are not the primary responsibility of their division
   D. considered reserve equipment

10. Of the following, the BEST example of the type of emergency referred to in the above   10.____
    paragraph is a(n)

    A. fireman injured at a fire and requiring transportation
    B. subway strike which prevents firemen from reporting for duty
    C. unusually large number of false alarms occurring at one time
    D. need for additional manpower at a fire

11. A *central assembly point*, as used in the above paragraph, would MOST likely be a place   11.____

    A. close to the place of the emergency
    B. in the geographical center of the division
    C. easily reached by the members assigned
    D. readily accessible to the intersection of major highways

Questions 12-14.

DIRECTIONS: Questions 12 through 14 are to be answered SOLELY on the basis of the following paragraph.

A plastic does not consist of a single substance, but is a blended combination of several.
In addition to the resin, it may contain various fillers, plasticizers, lubricants, and coloring
material. Depending upon the type and quantity of substances added to the binder, the properties, including combustibility, may be altered considerably. The flammability of plastics
depends upon the composition and, as with other materials, upon their physical size and condition. Thin sections, sharp edges, or powdered plastics will ignite and burn more readily than
the same amount of identical material in heavy sections with smooth surfaces.

12.   The one of the following conclusions that is BEST supported by the above paragraph is   12.
that the flammability of plastics

    A.   generally is high   B.   generally is moderate
    C.   generally is low   D.   varies considerably

13.   According to the above paragraph, *plastics* can BEST be described as   13.

    A.   a trade name
    B.   the name of a specific product
    C.   the name of a group of products which have some similar and some dissimilar
properties
    D.   the name of any substance which can be shaped or molded during the production
process

14.   According to the above paragraph, all plastics contain a   14.

    A.   resin
    B.   resin and a filler
    C.   resin, filler, and plasticizer
    D.   resin, filler, plasticizer, lubricant, and coloring material

Questions 15-18.

DIRECTIONS: Questions 15 through 18 are to be answered SOLELY on the basis of the following paragraph.

To guard against overheating of electrical conductors in buildings, an overcurrent protective device is provided for each circuit. This device is designed to open the circuit and cut off
the flow of current whenever the current exceeds a predetermined limit. The fuse, which is the
most common form of overcurrent protection, consists of a fusible metal element which when
heated by the current to a certain temperature melts and opens the circuit.

15.   According to the above paragraph, a circuit which is NOT carrying an electric current is   15.
a(n)

    A.   open circuit
    B.   closed circuit
    C.   circuit protected by a fuse
    D.   circuit protected by an overcurrent protective device other than a fuse

16. As used in the above paragraph, the one of the following which is the BEST example of a   16.____
conductor is a(n)

    A. metal table which comes in contact with a source of electricity
    B. storage battery generating electricity
    C. electrical wire carrying an electrical current
    D. dynamo converting mechanical energy into electrical energy

17. A fuse is NOT   17.____

    A. an overcurrent protective device
    B. the most common form of overcurrent protection
    C. dangerous because it allows such a strong flow of electricity that the wires carrying it may become heated enough to set fire to materials in contact with them
    D. a safety valve

18. According to the above paragraph, the MAXIMUM number of circuits that can be handled   18.____
by a fuse box containing 6 fuses

    A. is 3
    B. is 6
    C. is 12
    D. cannot be determined from the information given in the above Paragraph

Questions 19-21.

DIRECTIONS: Questions 19 through 21 are to be answered SOLELY on the basis of the following paragraph.

    Unlined linen hose is essentially a fabric tube made of closely woven linen yarn. Due to the natural characteristics of linen, very shortly after water is introduced, the threads swell after being wet, closing the minute spaces between them making the tube practically water tight. This type of hose tends to deteriorate rapidly if not thoroughly dried after use or if installed where it will be exposed to dampness or the weather. It is not ordinarily built to withstand frequent service or for use where the fabric will be subjected to chafing from rough or sharp surfaces.

19. Seepage of water through an unlined linen hose is observed when the water is first   19.____
turned on.
From the above paragraph, we may conclude that the seepage

    A. indicates that the hose is defective
    B. does not indicate that the hose is defective provided that the seepage is proportionate to the water pressure
    C. does not indicate that the hose is defective provided that the seepage is greatly reduced when the hose becomes thoroughly wet
    D. does not indicate that the hose is defective provided that the seepage takes place only at the surface of the hose

20. Unlined linen hose is MOST suitable for use

    A. as a garden hose
    B. on fire department apparatus
    C. as emergency fire equipment in buildings
    D. in fire department training schools

21. The use of unlined linen hose would be LEAST appropriate in a(n)

    A. outdoor lumber yard
    B. non-fireproof office building
    C. department store
    D. cosmetic manufacturing plant

Questions 22-25.

DIRECTIONS: Questions 22 through 25 are to be answered SOLELY on the basis of the following paragraph.

The velocity of moving water droplets decreases because of aerodynamic drag forces and gravitational effects. In the case of droplets of the sizes more favorable for fire extinguishment, these aerodynamic drag forces, opposing the motion of the droplets, are proportional to the square of the diameters of the droplets and to the square of their velocity. If the initial velocity of the droplets leaving the spray nozzles is resolved into a horizontal and vertical component, the aerodynamic drag affects the horizontal component, and both the aerodynamic drag and gravitation affect the vertical component. In still air, the horizontal velocity of a moving droplet approaches zero. The vertical velocity of the droplet approaches the terminal velocity of a free falling body, which is attained when the aerodynamic drag forces are in equilibrium with the weight of the droplet. The terminal velocity represents the lower limit of the relative velocity of water drops in air. From the standpoint of fire fighting, the absolute velocity of the moving drops is also important, since the horizontal component of the absolute velocity must be sufficient for the droplets to reach the heated area surrounding the fire, and to penetrate the updraft to the seat of the fire.

22. The one of the following forces which would contribute MOST to *aerodynamic drag forces*, as that term is used in the above paragraph, is

    A. friction   B. gravity   C. inertia   D. momentum

22

23. Assume that water droplets in one stream have four times the diameter and the same initial velocity as droplets in a second stream.
    From the above paragraph, we may conclude that the aerodynamic drag forces on the first stream, compared to the second, initially are _____ as much.

    A. twice   B. four times
    C. eight times   D. sixteen times

24. The horizontal velocity of a moving droplet approaches zero when the

    A. horizontal velocity approaches the terminal velocity of a free falling body
    B. square of the diameter of the droplet is proportional to the square of the velocity of the droplet
    C. vertical velocity is in equilibrium with the aerodynamic drag forces
    D. maximum horizontal reach of the stream is obtained

25. The relative velocity of water droplets is equal to the absolute velocity when   25.____

    A. aerodynamic drag forces are in equilibrium with the weight of the droplets
    B. the square of the diameter of the droplets is proportional to the square of the velocity
    C. the air through which the droplets pass is still
    D. the aerodynamic drag forces equal the gravitational effects on the droplets

---

KEY (CORRECT ANSWERS)

1. B	11. C		
2. B	12. D		
3. B	13. C		
4. C	14. A		
5. C	15. A		
6. A	16. A		
7. B	17. C		
8. B	18. B		
9. A	19. C		
10. D	20. C		

21. A
22. A
23. D
24. D
25. C

TEST 2

Questions 1-4.

DIRECTIONS: Questions 1 through 4 are to be answered SOLELY on the basis of the following paragraph.

During fire operations, all members shall be constantly alert to possibility of the crime of
arson. In the event conditions indicate this possibility, the officer in command shall promptly
notify the Fire Marshal. Unauthorized persons shall be prohibited from entering premises and
actions of those authorized carefully noted. Members shall refrain from discussion of the fire
and prevent disturbance of essential evidence. If necessary, the officer in command shall
detail one or more members at location with information for the Fire Marshal upon his arrival.

1. From the above paragraph, it may be inferred that the reason for prohibiting unauthorized   1.___
    persons from entering the fire premises when arson is suspected is to prevent such per-
    sons from

    A.   endangering themselves in the fire
    B.   interfering with the firemen fighting the fire
    C.   disturbing any evidence of arson
    D.   committing acts of arson

2. The one of the following titles which BEST describes the subject matter of the above   2.___
    paragraph is

    A.   TECHNIQUES OF ARSON DETECTION
    B.   THE ROLE OF THE FIRE MARSHAL IN ARSON CASES
    C.   FIRE SCENE PROCEDURES IN CASES OF SUSPECTED ARSON
    D.   EVIDENCE IN ARSON INVESTIGATIONS

3. The one of the following statements that is MOST correct and complete is that the   3.___
    responsibility for detecting signs of arson at a fire belongs to the

    A.   Fire Marshal
    B.   Fire Marshal and officer in command
    C.   Fire Marshal, officer in command, and any members detailed at location with infor-
         mation for the Fire Marshal
    D.   members present at the scene of the fire regardless of their rank or position

4. From the above paragraph, it may be inferred that the Fire Marshal USUALLY arrives at   4.___
    the scene of a fire

    A.   before the fire companies
    B.   simultaneously with the fire companies
    C.   immediately after the fire companies
    D.   some time after the fire companies

Questions 5-8.

DIRECTIONS: Questions 5 through 8 are to be answered SOLELY on the basis of the following paragraph.

FIRES

The four types of fires are called Class A, Class B, Class C, and Class D. Examples of Class A fires are paper, cloth, or wood fires. The types of extinguishers used on Class A fires are foam, soda acid, or water. Class B fires are those in burning liquids. They require a smothering action for extinguishment. Carbon dioxide, dry chemical, vaporizing liquid, or foam are the types of extinguishers that are used on burning liquids. Electrical fires, such as in motors and switches, are Class C fires. A non-conducting extinguishing agent must be used for this kind of fire. Therefore, carbon dioxide, dry chemical, or vaporizing liquid extinguishers are used. Fires in motor vehicles are Class D fires; and carbon dioxide, dry chemical, or vaporizing liquid extinguishers should be used on them.

5. According to the information in the above paragraph, a fire in a can full of gasoline would be a Class _____ fire.   5._____

   A. D   B. C   C. B   D. A

6. In the above paragraph, the extinguishers recommended are entirely the same for Class _____ and Class _____ fires.   6._____

   A. B; D   B. C; D   C. B; C   D. A; B

7. According to the information in the above paragraph, a water extinguisher would MOST likely be suitable for use on which one of the following fires? A(n)   7._____

   A. fire in a truck engine
   B. fire in an electrical switch
   C. oil fire
   D. lumber fire

8. According to the information in the above paragraph, dry chemical   8._____

   A. should NOT be used on a burning liquid fire
   B. is a conducting extinguishing agent
   C. should NOT be used on a fire in a car
   D. smothers fires to put them out

Questions 9-10.

DIRECTIONS: Questions 9 and 10 are to be answered SOLELY on the basis of the following passage.

One of the greatest hazards to an industrial plant is fire. Consequently, a rigid system should be set up for periodic inspection of all types of fire protective equipment. Such inspections should include water tanks, sprinkler systems, standpipes, hose, fire plugs, extinguishers, and all other equipment used for fire protection. The schedule of inspections should be closely followed and an *accurate* record kept of each piece of equipment inspected and tested.

Along with this scheduled inspection, a careful survey should be made of new equipment needed. Recommendations should be made for replacement of defective and obsolete equipment, as well as the purchase of any additional equipment. As new processes and products are added to the manufacturing system, new fire hazards may be introduced that require individual treatment and possible special extinguishing devices. Plant inspection personnel should be sure to follow through.

Surveys should also include all means of egress from the building. Exits, stairs, fire towers, fire escapes, halls, fire alarm systems, emergency lighting systems, and places seldom used should be thoroughly inspected to determine their adequacy and readiness for emergency use.

9. Of the following titles, the one that BEST fits the above passage is 9._

    A. NEW, USED, AND OLD FIRE PROTECTION EQUIPMENT
    B. MAINTENANCE OF FIRE PROTECTION EQUIPMENT
    C. INSPECTION OF FIRE PROTECTION EQUIPMENT
    D. OVERHAUL OF WORN OUT FIRE FIGHTING EQUIPMENT

10. As used in the above passage, the word *accurate* means 10._

    A. exact   B. approximate   C. close   D. vague

Questions 11-15.

DIRECTIONS: Questions 11 through 15 are to be answered SOLELY on the basis of the following passage.

The sizes of living rooms shall meet the following requirements:

    a. In each apartment, there shall be at least one living room containing at least 120 square feet of clear floor area, and every other living room except a kitchen shall contain at least 70 square feet of clear floor area.
    b. Every living room which contains less than 80 square feet of clear floor area or which is located in the cellar or basement shall be at least 9 feet high and every other living room 8 feet high.

Apartments containing three or more rooms may have dining bays, which shall not exceed 55 square feet in floor surface area and shall not be deemed separate rooms or subject to the requirements for separate rooms. Every such dining bay shall be provided with at least one window containing an area at least one-eighth of the floor surface area of such dining bay.

11. The MINIMUM volume of a living room, other than a kitchen, which meets the minimum requirements of the above paragraph is one that measures _____ cubic feet. 11._

    A. 70   B. 80   C. 630   D. 640

12. A builder proposes to construct an apartment house containing an apartment consisting of a kitchen which measures 10 feet by 6 feet, a room 12 feet by 12 feet, and one 11 feet by 7 feet.
This apartment 12._

    A. does not comply with the requirements of the above paragraph
    B. complies with the requirements of the above paragraph provided that it is not located in the cellar or basement

C.   complies with the requirements of the above paragraph provided that the height of the smaller rooms is at least 9 feet
D.   may or may not comply with the requirements of the above paragraph, depending upon the clear floor area of the kitchen

13. The one of the following definitions of the term *living room* which is MOST in accord with its meaning in the above paragraph is

    13._____

    A.   a sitting room or parlor
    B.   the largest room in an apartment
    C.   a room used for living purposes
    D.   any room in an apartment containing 120 square feet of clear floor Area

14. Assume that one room in a four-room apartment measures 20 feet by 10 feet and contains a dining bay 8 feet by 6 feet. According to the above passage, the dining bay MUST be provided with a window measuring AT LEAST _____ square feet.

    14._____

    A.   6   B.   7   C.   25   D.   55

15. Kitchens, according to the above passage, are

    15._____

    A.   not considered *living rooms*
    B.   considered *living rooms* and must, therefore, meet the height and area requirements of the paragraph
    C.   considered *living rooms* but they need not meet either the height or area requirements of the paragraph
    D.   considered *living rooms* but they need meet only the height requirements, not the area requirements, of the paragraph

Questions 16-20.

DIRECTIONS: Questions 16 through 20 are to be answered SOLELY on the basis of the following paragraph.

Cotton fabrics treated with the XYZ Process have features which make them far superior to any previously known flame-retardant-treated cotton fabrics. XYZ are glow resistant; when exposed to flames or intense heat form tough, pliable, and protective chars; are inert physiologically to persons handling or exposed to the fabric; are only slightly heavier than untreated fabrics; and are susceptible to further wet and dry finishing treatments. In addition, the treated fabrics exhibit little or no adverse change in feel, texture, and appearance, and are shrink-, rot-, and mildew-resistant. The treatment reduces strength only slightly. Finished fabrics have *easy care* properties in that they are wrinkle-resistant and dry rapidly.

16. It is MOST accurate to state that the author, in the above paragraph, presents

    16._____

    A.   facts but reaches no conclusion concerning the value of the process
    B.   his conclusion concerning the value of the process and facts to support his conclusion
    C.   his conclusion concerning the value of the process unsupported by facts
    D.   neither facts nor conclusions, but merely describes the process

17. The one of the following articles for which the XYZ Process would be MOST suitable is   17.__

    A. nylon stockings   B. woolen shirt
    C. silk tie   D. cotton bedsheet

18. The one of the following aspects of the XYZ Process which is NOT discussed in the   18.__
above paragraph is its effects on

    A. costs   B. washability
    C. wearability   D. the human body

19. The MAIN reason for treating a fabric with the XYZ Process is to   19.__

    A. prepare the fabric for other wet and dry finishing treatments
    B. render it shrink-, rot-, and mildew-resistant
    C. increase its weight and strength
    D. reduce the chance that it will catch fire

20. The one of the following which would be considered a MINOR drawback of the XYZ Pro-   20.__
cess is that it

    A. forms chars when exposed to flame
    B. makes fabrics mildew-resistant
    C. adds to the weight of fabrics
    D. is compatible with other finishing treatments

Questions 21-25.

DIRECTIONS: Questions 21 through 25 are to be answered SOLELY on the basis of the following paragraph.

    In order to help prevent the spread of fire, it is necessary to understand the means by
which heat is transmitted. Heat is transmitted through solids by a method called *conduction*.
Materials vary greatly in their ability to transmit heat. Metals are good conductors of heat. On
the other hand, wood, glass, pottery, asbestos, and many like substances are very poor conductors of heat and are termed insulators. It should be remembered, however, that there are
no perfect insulators of heat. All will conduct heat to some extent; and if the heat continues
long enough, it will be transmitted through the solid. The hazard of heat transmission is illus-
trated by the fact that a fire on one side of a metal wall could start a fire on the other side if
combustibles were close to the wall.

21. Of the following, the BEST material to use for the handle of a metal pan to guard against   21.__
heat is

    A. copper   B. iron   C. wood   D. steel

22. According to the above paragraph, *conduction* applies to the traveling of heat through a   22.__

    A. solid   B. liquid
    C. slow-moving fluid   D. gas

23. According to the information in the above paragraph, when storing combustible materials in a room with metal walls, it is BEST to 23._____

   A. keep the combustibles close together
   B. keep the combustibles away from the metal walls
   C. put the non-metals nearest the metal walls
   D. separate metal materials from non-metal materials

24. Based on the information in the above paragraph, which one of the following objects is the BEST conductor of heat? 24._____

   A. Pottery   B. An oak desk
   C. A glass jar   D. A silver spoon

25. Of the following, the title which BEST describes what the above paragraph is about is 25._____

   A. USES OF CONDUCTORS AND INSULATORS
   B. THE REASONS WHY FIRE SPREADS
   C. HEAT TRANSMISSION AND FIRES
   D. THE HAZARDS OF POOR CONDUCTION

KEY (CORRECT ANSWERS)

1. C		11. C	
2. C		12. C	
3. D		13. C	
4. D		14. A	
5. C		15. D	
6. B		16. B	
7. D		17. D	
8. D		18. A	
9. C		19. D	
10. A		20. C	

21. C
22. A
23. B
24. D
25. C

WORD MEANING
EXAMINATION SECTION
TEST 1

DIRECTIONS: Each question or incomplete statement is followed by several suggested answers or completions. Select the one that BEST answers the question or completes the statement. *PRINT THE LETTER OF THE CORRECT ANSWER IN THE SPACE AT THE RIGHT.*

1. In the sentence, *Malice was immanent in all his remarks,* the word *immanent* means MOST NEARLY

    A. elevated   B. inherent
    C. threatening   D. foreign

1.____

2. In the sentence, *The extant copies of the document were found in the safe,* the word *extant* means MOST NEARLY

    A. existing   B. original
    C. forged   D. duplicate

2.____

3. In the sentence, *The recruit was more complaisant after the captain spoke to him,* the word *complaisant* means MOST NEARLY

    A. calm   B. affable
    C. irritable   D. confident

3.____

4. In the sentence, *The man was captured under highly creditable circumstances,* the word *creditable* means MOST NEARLY

    A. doubtful   B. believable
    C. praiseworthy   D. unexpected

4.____

5. In the sentence, *His superior officers were more sagacious than he,* the word *sagacious* means MOST NEARLY

    A. shrewd   B. obtuse   C. absurd   D. verbose

5.____

6. In the sentence, *He spoke with impunity,* the word *impunity* means MOST NEARLY

    A. rashness   B. caution
    C. without fear   D. immunity

6.____

7. In the sentence, *The new patrolman displayed unusual temerity during the emergency,* the word *temerity* means MOST NEARLY

    A. fear   B. rashness   C. calmness   D. anxiety

7.____

8. In the sentence, *The portions of food were parsimoniously served,* the word *parsimoniously* means MOST NEARLY

    A. stingily   B. piously
    C. elaborately   D. generously

8.____

9. In the sentence, *Generally the speaker's remarks were sententious,* the word *sententious* means MOST NEARLY

    A. verbose
    B. witty
    C. argumentative
    D. pithy

10. In the sentence, *The prisoner was fractious when brought to the station house,* the word *fractious* means MOST NEARLY

    A. penitent
    B. talkative
    C. irascible
    D. broken-hearted

11. In the sentence, *The judge was implacable when the attorney pleaded for leniency,* the word *implacable* means MOST NEARLY

    A. inexorable
    B. disinterested
    C. inattentive
    D. indifferent

12. In the sentence, *The court ordered the mendacious statements stricken from the record,* the word *mendacious* means MOST NEARLY

    A. begging
    B. lying
    C. threatening
    D. lengthy

13. In the sentence, *The district attorney spoke in a strident voice,* the word *strident* means MOST NEARLY

    A. loud
    B. harsh-sounding
    C. sing-song
    D. low

14. In the sentence, *The speaker had a predilection for long sentences,* the word *predilection* means MOST NEARLY

    A. aversion
    B. talent
    C. propensity
    D. diffidence

15. A section of the Penal Law states that *a morbid propensity to commit prohibited acts.... forms no defense to a prosecution therefor.*
The word *propensity* as used in this statute means MOST NEARLY

    A. capacity   B. ability   C. tendency   D. aptitude

16. A police department rule provides that a *Chaplain shall have the assimilated rank of Inspector.*
The word *assimilated* as used in this rule means MOST NEARLY

    A. false
    B. superior
    C. comparable
    D. presumed

17. A police department rule provides that *Pushcarts and derelict automobiles shall be delivered to the Bureau of Incumbrances.*
The word *derelict* as used in this rule means MOST NEARLY

    A. dilapidated
    B. abandoned
    C. delinquent
    D. contraband

18. A police department rule provides that *when the exigencies of the service shall so require, a captain may assign a patrolman from the outgoing platoon to house duty.* The word *exigencies* as used in this rule means MOST NEARLY

    A. needs   B. conveniences
    C. changes   D. increases

18._____

19. A police department rule provides for the award of a Medal for Merit *for an act of outstanding bravery, performed in the line of duty, at imminent personal hazard of life.* The word *imminent* as used in this rule means MOST NEARLY

    A. impending   B. inherent   C. certain   D. great

19._____

20. A police department rule provides that *the Police Commissioner shall have cognizance and control of the government, administration, disposition and discipline of the Police Department.* The word *cognizance* as used in this rule means MOST NEARLY

    A. responsibility for   B. jurisdiction over
    C. knowledge of   D. ability for

20._____

21. A police department rule provides that a member of the department shall not communicate with a railroad company *for the purpose of expediting the issue of a transportation pass.* The word *expediting* as used in this rule means MOST NEARLY

    A. extorting   B. procuring
    C. demanding   D. hastening

21._____

22. A section of the Penal Law provides, in part, that *whenever the punishment or penalty for an offense is mitigated by any provision of this chapter, such provision may be applied to any sentence or judgment imposed for the offense.* The word *mitigated* as used in this statute means MOST NEARLY

    A. removed   B. augmented
    C. changed   D. decreased

22._____

23. A Police Department Manual of Procedure provides that a member of the force who comes into possession of a document containing scurrilous matter will take precautions to safeguard fingerprints thereon. The word *scurrilous* as used in this regulation means MOST NEARLY

    A. irrelevant   B. offensive
    C. defamatory   D. evidentiary

23._____

24. Under cases of *Mendicancy* should be listed cases of

    A. loitering   B. begging
    C. carrying of weapons   D. injury to property

24._____

25. A police department rule states that *the Department Medal of Honor may be awarded to a member of the Force who distinguishes himself by an act of gallantry and intrepidity.* The word *intrepidity* as used in this rule means MOST NEARLY

    A. chivalry   B. virility   C. fear   D. courage

25._____

KEY (CORRECT ANSWERS)

1.	B		11.	A
2.	A		12.	B
3.	B		13.	B
4.	C		14.	C
5.	A		15.	C
6.	D		16.	C
7.	B		17.	B
8.	A		18.	A
9.	D		19.	A
10.	C		20.	C

21. D
22. D
23. B
24. B
25. D

———

TEST 2

DIRECTIONS: Each question or incomplete statement is followed by several suggested
answers or completions. Select the one that BEST answers the question or
completes the statement. *PRINT THE LETTER OF THE CORRECT ANSWER
IN THE SPACE AT THE RIGHT.*

1. A foreman who <u>expedites</u> a job   1._____

    A.   abolishes it   B.   makes it bigger
    C.   slows it down   D.   speeds it up

2. If a man is working at a <u>uniform</u> speed, it means he is working at a speed which is   2._____

    A.   changing   B.   fast   C.   slow   D.   steady

3. To say that a caretaker is <u>obstinate</u> means that he is   3._____

    A.   cooperative   B.   patient
    C.   stubborn   D.   willing

4. To say that a caretaker is <u>negligent</u> means that he is   4._____

    A.   careless   B.   neat   C.   nervous   D.   late

5. To say that something is <u>absurd</u> means that it is   5._____

    A.   definite   B.   not clear
    C.   ridiculous   D.   unfair

6. To say that a foreman is <u>impartial</u> means that he is   6._____

    A.   fair   B.   improving
    C.   in a hurry   D.   watchful

7. A foreman who is <u>lenient</u> is one who is   7._____

    A.   careless   B.   harsh
    C.   inexperienced   D.   mild

8. A foreman who is <u>punctual</u> is one who is   8._____

    A.   able   B.   polite   C.   prompt   D.   sincere

9. If you think one of your men is too <u>awkward</u> to do a job, it means you think he is too   9._____

    A.   clumsy   B.   lazy   C.   old   D.   weak

10. A man who is <u>seldom</u> late is late   10._____

    A.   always   B.   never   C.   often   D.   rarely

Questions 11-18.

DIRECTIONS: In Questions 11 through 18, select the choice that is CLOSEST in meaning to the underlined word.

11. A central file eliminates the need to <u>retain</u> duplicate material.   11.___

   A. keep   B. change   C. locate   D. process

12. Filing is a <u>routine</u> office task.   12.___

   A. proper   B. regular   C. simple   D. difficult

13. Sometimes a word, phrase, or sentence must be <u>deleted</u> to correct an error.   13.___

   A. removed   B. added   C. expanded   D. improved

14. Your supervisor will <u>evaluate</u> your work.   14.___

   A. judge   B. list   C. assign   D. explain

15. Railroad Clerks must <u>ascertain</u> the identification of all individuals claiming to be Transit Authority employees.   15.___

   A. observe   B. record   C. challenge   D. verify

16. A Railroad Clerk must not permit anyone to <u>loiter</u> near his booth.   16.___

   A. throw refuse   B. smoke
   C. stand idly   D. make noise

17. The Transit Authority has a program for eliminating <u>graffiti</u> in subway cars.   17.___

   A. noise   B. markings
   C. vandalism   D. debris

18. The Railroad Clerk will <u>deduct</u> the number of tokens she sold from the number of tokens she had in reserve when she started her tour of duty.   18.___

   A. add   B. subtract   C. multiply   D. divide

Questions 19-30.

DIRECTIONS: Questions 19 through 30 contain incorrectly used words which change the meaning of the statement. Identify the word in the statement that is incorrect and select the choice that would make the sentence correct.

19. Lack of employee input in the case of training often exists, but is frequently dealt with in evaluation of the training effort. Failure to deal with as important a factor as this can be ruinous to the training effort.   19.___

   A. Seldom   B. Margin
   C. Ancillary   D. Contributory

20. It is a fallacy that policies generated at the top of the hierarchy are often not acceptable to those on the lower levels, particularly in the case of blue-collar workers among whom the rewards and sanctions of the union or members of the immediate social group are more impelling than the rewards or sanctions available to management.   20.____

   A. Parologism   B. Truism
   C. Commands   D. Undetermined

21. Basically, an organization develops when employees in it have rather free control over their behavior within the organization, when the philosophy of the organization is that maximum interpersonal interplay through a minimum number of hierarchical levels is desirable, and when a person traditionally called a *trainer* performs an integrating function.   21.____

   A. Instinctively   B. Total
   C. Flat   D. Strong

22. In gaining cooperation in human relations, the one who would influence must often foster his own ego and fertilize and feed that of the one who is to be influenced.   22.____

   A. Lassitude   B. Emulate
   C. Suppress   D. Implant

23. In the United States, in general, we have been criticized for our emphasis upon physical, materialistic, and economic goals. These are still important, but the trends point toward the more complex, or appreciation of the beautiful, as for example in the architecture of our new factories and colors in the workplaces.   23.____

   A. Ephemeral   B. Concrete   C. Prosaic   D. Aesthetic

24. Standards of production performance are necessary to reveal the quantities of material, the number of hours of labor, the machine hours, and quantities of service (as, for example, power, steam, etc.) necessary to perform the various production operations. The establishment of such standards is an engineering rather than an accounting task, but it should be emphasized that such standards are needless to the development of the budgetary procedure at least insofar as the budget is to serve as a tool of control. Such standards serve not only in the development of the budget and in measuring efficiency of production performance, but also in developing purchase requirements and in estimating costs.   24.____

   A. Manifest   B. Evaluation
   C. Essential   D. Function

25. Where standard costs are not available or their use is impracticable due to uncertainty of prices, estimates of the costs must be made on the basis of past experience and expected conditions. Ability to use standards largely eliminates the use of the budget for purposes of control of costs but its value remains for purposes of coordination of the program with purchases and finance.   25.____

   A. Failure   B. Current
   C. Culmination   D. Apparent

26. While one of the first objectives of the labor budget is to provide the highest practicable degree of regularity of employment, consideration must also be given to the estimating and perdurability of labor cost. Regularity of employment in itself effects some reduction in labor cost, but when carried beyond the point of practicability, it may increase other costs. For example, additional sales effort may be required to expand sales volume or to develop new products for slack periods; the cost of carrying inventories and the dangers of obsolescence and price declines must also be considered. A proper balance must be secured.

   26.___

  A.   Material   B.   Control   C.   Futures   D. To

27. The essentials of budgeting perhaps can be summarized in this manner:
 1. Develop a sound business program.
 2. Report on the progress in achieving that program.
 3. Take necessary action as to all variances which are inevitable.
 4. Revise the program to meet the changing conditions as required.

   27.___

  A.   Perfect   B.   Plans
  C.   Controllable   D.   Secure

28. If a planning and control procedure is considered worthwhile, then it is a syllogism that preparation for the installation should be adequate. Time devoted to this educational aspect ordinarily will prove quite rewarding. The management to be involved with the budget, and particularly the middle management, must have a clear understanding of the budgetary procedure.

   28.___

  A.   Acquired   B.   Remedial   C.   Monetary   D.   Truism

29. Among the Housing Manager's overall responsibilities in administering a project is the prevention of the development of conditions which might lead to termination of tenancy and eviction of a tenant. Where there appears to be doubt that a tenant is fully aware of his responsibilities and is thus jeopardizing his tenancy, the Housing Manager should acquaint him with these responsibilities. Where a situation involves behavior of a tenant or a member of his family, the Housing Manager should confirm, through discussions and referrals to social agencies, correction of the conditions before they reach a state where there is no alternative but termination proceedings.

   29.___

  A.   Coordinate   B.   Identify
  C.   Assert   D.   Attempt

30. The one universal administrative complaint is that the budget is inadequate. Between adequacy and inadequacy lie all degrees of adequacy. Further, human wants are modest in relation to human resources. From these two facts we may conclude that the fundamental criterion of administrative decision must be a criterion of efficiency (the degree to which the goals have been reached relative to the available resources) rather than a criterion of adequacy (the degree to which its goals have been reached). The task of the manager is to maximize social values relative to limited resources.

   30.___

  A.   Improve   B.   Simple
  C.   Limitless   D.   Optimize

KEY (CORRECT ANSWERS)

1.	D		16.	C
2.	D		17.	B
3.	C		18.	B
4.	A		19.	A
5.	C		20.	B
6.	A		21.	D
7.	D		22.	C
8.	C		23.	D
9.	A		24.	C
10.	D		25.	B
11.	A		26.	B
12.	B		27.	C
13.	A		28.	D
14.	A		29.	D
15.	D		30.	C

———

WORD MEANING

EXAMINATION SECTION
TEST 1

DIRECTIONS : For the following questions, select the word or group of words lettered A, B, C, D, or E that means MOST NEARLY the same as the word in capital letters. *PRINT THE LETTER OF THE CORRECT ANSWER IN THE SPACE AT THE RIGHT.*

1. PERHAPS you misunderstood his instructions. PERHAPS means *most nearly*   1.____

    A. at least   B. happily   C. maybe   D. of course   E. surely

2. Do you think the exhibit MERITS an award? MERITS means *most nearly*   2.____

    A. deserves   B. gets   C. lacks   D. requires   E. wins

3. It was a very UNUSUAL day for April. UNUSUAL means *most nearly*   3.____

    A. cold   B. delightful   C. good   D. ordinary   E. rare

4. A single FRAGRANT rose decorated his desk. FRAGRANT means *most nearly*   4.____

    A. late-blooming   B. rambling   C. sweet-smelling
    D. wilted   E. yellow

5. The GLITTERING bead attracted the crow. GLITTERING means *most nearly*   5.____

    A. bouncing   B. colored   C. gleaming   D. pretty   E. rolling

6. Jack did NOTICE the attractive child. NOTICE means *most nearly*   6.____

    A. believe   B. observe   C. overlook   D. speak to   E. write to

7. We are too fond of the ADVANTAGES of civilization. ADVANTAGES means *most nearly*   7.____

    A. benefits   B. changes   C. classes   D. powers   E. results

8. Accidents in the home may cause INJURY. INJURY means *most nearly*   8.____

    A. danger   B. death   C. delay   D. grief   E. harm

9. The Spanish explorers found great TREASURES for their king. TREASURES means *most nearly*   9.____

    A. banks   B. chests   C. islands   D. riches   E. values

10. They prepared a great BANQUET for the returning general. BANQUET means *most nearly*   10.____

    A. ball   B. feast   C. gift   D. hall   E. surprise

11. We must learn to be TOLERANT of people different from ourselves. TOLERANT means *most nearly*   11.____

    A. afraid   B. aware   C. careful   D. suspicious
    E. understanding

12. His AMBITION caused him to go to night school. AMBITION means *most nearly*   12.__

    A. desire to succeed   B. fortune   C. hope of freedom
    D. ignorance   E. pride

13. The frightened child ran to EMBRACE her mother. EMBRACE means *most nearly*   13.__

    A. call   B. escape   C. hug   D. scold   E. watch

14. ACTUALLY he did not know the man. ACTUALLY means *most nearly*   14.__

    A. now   B. often   C. really   D. suddenly   E. then

15. The hike up Mount Marcy was STRENUOUS. STRENUOUS means *most nearly*   15.__

    A. disappointing   B. dull   C. pleasant
    D. scenic   E. vigorous

KEY (CORRECT ANSWERS)

1.	C		6.	B
2.	A		7.	A
3.	E		8.	E
4.	C		9.	D
5.	C		10.	B

11.	E
12.	A
13.	C
14.	C
15.	E

TEST 2

DIRECTIONS : For the following questions, select the word or group of words lettered A, B, C, D, or E that means MOST NEARLY the same as the word in capital letters. *PRINT THE LETTER OF THE CORRECT ANSWER IN THE SPACE AT THE RIGHT.*

1. The traveler carried SUFFICIENT money for the trip. SUFFICIENT means *most nearly*   1.____

   A. counterfeit   B. enough   C. less
   D. too little   E. too much

2. He walked HASTILY to the counter. HASTILY means *most nearly*   2.____

   A. angrily   B. often   C. quickly   D. seldom   E. slowly

3. I shall CONCEAL the letter in the tree. CONCEAL means *most nearly*   3.____

   A. catch   B. find   C. hide   D. steal   E. throw

4. He prefers to DWELL in the country. DWELL means *most nearly*   4.____

   A. build   B. picnic   C. rent   D. live   E. continue

5. There is no CERTAIN way of locating their treasure. CERTAIN means *most nearly*   5.____

   A. better   B. easy   C. familiar   D. private   E. sure

6. In FORMER times life was more simple. FORMER means *most nearly*   6.____

   A. better   B. later   C. earlier   D. happier   E. calmer

7. The immigrant's arrival marked the COMMENCEMENT of a new life. COMMENCEMENT means *most nearly*   7.____

   A. beginning   B. choosing   C. finishing   D. seeking   E. settling

8. The war brought the people much MISERY. MISERY means *most nearly*   8.____

   A. distress   B. distrust   C. toil   D. hatred   E. money

9. The teacher was EXTREMELY pleased with her students. EXTREMELY means *most nearly*   9.____

   A. seldom   B. often   C. sometimes   D. frequently   E. very

10. The trapper INDICATED the streams where fishing was best. INDICATED means *most nearly*   10.____

    A. described   B. kept secret   C. pointed out
    D. retraced   E. walked along

11. The odd results of the experiment PERPLEXED the scientists. PERPLEXED means *most nearly*   11.____

    A. decided   B. disgusted   C. helped   D. puzzled   E. surprised

12. The hostess greeted the guest CORDIALLY. CORDIALLY means *most nearly*   12.___

    A. unpleasantly   B. coldly   C. crudely   D. heartily
    E. sentimentally

13. Do not CONFUSE the audience when you speak. CONFUSE means *most nearly*   13.___

    A. tire   B. bewilder   C. consider   D. criticize   E. forget

14. The HOSTILE attitude of my neighbor frightened me. HOSTILE means *most nearly*   14.___

    A. doubtful   B. friendly   C. indifferent
    D. suspicious   E. unfriendly

15. How long do you think you can ENDURE these conditions? ENDURE means *most nearly*   15.___

    A. await   B. bear   C. demand   D. escape   E. obey

KEY (CORRECT ANSWERS)

1.	B		6.	C
2.	C		7.	A
3.	C		8.	A
4.	D		9.	E
5.	E		10.	C

11.	D
12.	D
13.	B
14.	E
15.	B

TEST 3

DIRECTIONS : For the following questions, select the word or group of words lettered A, B, C, D, or E that means MOST NEARLY the same as the word in capital letters. *PRINT THE LETTER OF THE CORRECT ANSWER IN THE SPACE AT THE RIGHT.*

1. The office manager was given considerable LATITUDE insetting up the procedures for the new unit. LATITUDE means *most nearly*   1.____

   A. advice and encouragement
   C. cause for annoyance
   E. freedom from fear
   B. assistance and cooperation
   D. freedom from restriction

2. He said that this was an EXPEDIENT method of performing the job. EXPEDIENT means *most nearly*   2.____

   A. inconvenient and ineffective
   C. practical and efficient
   E. forceful but necessary
   B. effective but expensive
   D. convenient but time consuming

3. The men refused to give up their PREROGATIVES without a struggle. PREROGATIVES means *most nearly*   3.____

   A. ideals   B. demands   C. rights   D. advantages   E. exemptions

4. Shakespeare was a PROLIFIC writer. PROLIFIC means *most nearly*   4.____

   A. productive   B. popular   C. richly talented
   D. forward-looking   E. enigmatic

5. His electric lines are in close PROXIMITY with mine. PROXIMITY means *most nearly*   5.____

   A. nearness
   C. identity
   E. prolixity
   B. appropriateness
   D. necessity

6. The situation presented an unanticipated DILEMMA to the supervisor. DILEMMA means *most nearly*   6.____

   A. procedure
   C. opportunity
   E. predicament
   B. solution
   D. assignment

7. The population of a city is generally more HETEROGENEOUS than that of a rural community. HETEROGENEOUS means *most nearly*   7.____

   A. mixed   B. competent   C. unhealthy   D. prosperous   E. unique

8. His mother is a FRUGAL person. FRUGAL means *most nearly*   8.____

   A. discontented
   C. untruthful
   E. profound
   B. cheerful
   D. thrifty

9. Their interests were INIMICAL to the objectives of the organization. INIMICAL means *most nearly*   9.___

    A. opposed   B. agreeable   C. related   D. essential   E. unlike

10. He is an ECCENTRIC old man. ECCENTRIC means *most nearly*   10.___

    A. wealthy   B. self-centered
    C. envious   D. peculiar
    E. extravagant

11. The caller's manner was FURTIVE. FURTIVE means *most nearly*   11.___

    A. careless   B. sly   C. forceful   D. aloof   E. frivolous

12. The clerk CORROBORATED the stenographer's report. CORROBORATED means *most nearly*   12.___

    A. contradicted   B. confirmed
    C. summarized   D. corrected
    E. questioned

13. The manager dictated a TERSE letter. TERSE means *most nearly*   13.___

    A. angry   B. coherent   C. brief   D. lengthy   E. tearful

14. The EMINENT visitor drew all eyes. EMINENT means *most nearly*   14.___

    A. menacing   B. uninvited   C. awkward   D. tall   E. notable

15. Her quiet tone MITIGATED his anxiety. MITIGATED means *most nearly*   15.___

    A. intensified   B. alleviated   C. ridiculed   D. provoked   E. belied

---

KEY (CORRECT ANSWERS)

1.	D	6.	E
2.	C	7.	A
3.	C	8.	D
4.	A	9.	A
5.	A	10.	D

11.	B
12.	B
13.	C
14.	E
15.	B

TEST 4

DIRECTIONS : For the following questions, select the word or group of words lettered A, B, C, D, or E that means MOST NEARLY the same as the word in capital letters. *PRINT THE LETTER OF THE CORRECT ANSWER IN THE SPACE AT THE RIGHT.*

1. The extinguisher must be INVERTED before it will operate. INVERTED means *most nearly*   1.____

   A. turned over   B. completely filled   C. lightly shaken
   D. unhooked   E. opened

2. Sprinkler systems in buildings can RETARD the spread of fires. RETARD means *most nearly*   2.____

   A. quench   B. outline   C. slow   D. reveal   E. aggravate

3. Although there was widespread criticism, the director refused to CURTAIL the program. CURTAIL means *most nearly*   3.____

   A. change   B. discuss   C. shorten   D. expand   E. enforce

4. Argon is an INERT gas. INERT means *most nearly*   4.____

   A. unstable   B. uncommon C. volatile   D. inferior   E. inactive

5. The firemen turned their hoses on the shed and the main building SIMULTANEOUSLY. SIMULTANEOUSLY means *most nearly*   5.____

   A. in turn   B. without hesitation   C. with great haste
   D. as needed   E. at the same time

6. The officer was REBUKED for his failure to act promptly. REBUKED means *most nearly*   6.____

   A. demoted   B. reprimanded
   C. discharged   D. reassigned
   E. suspended

7. Parkways in the city may be used to FACILITATE responses to alarms. FACILITATE means *most nearly*   7.____

   A. reduce   B. alter   C. complete   D. ease   E. control

8. Fire extinguishers are most effective when the fire is INCIPIENT. INCIPIENT means *most nearly*   8.____

   A. accessible B. beginning C. red hot   D. confined   E. smoky

9. It is important to CONVEY TO new members the fundamental methods of firefighting. CONVEY TO means *most nearly*   9.____

   A. inquire of   B. prove for   C. confirm for
   D. suggest to   E. impart to

10. The explosion was a GRAPHIC illustration of the effects of neglect and carelessness. GRAPHIC means *most nearly*   10.____

   A. terrible   B. poor   C. typical   D. unique   E. vivid

11. The fireman was ASSIDUOUS in all things relating to his duties. ASSIDUOUS means *most nearly*   11.__

     A. aggressive   B. careless   C. persistent   D. cautious   E. dogmatic

12. A fireman must be ADEPT to be successful at his work. ADEPT means *most nearly*   12.__

     A. ambitious   B. strong   C. agile   D. alert   E. skillful

13. Officers shall see that parts are issued in CONSECUTIVE order. CONSECUTIVE means *most nearly*   13.__

     A. objective   B. random   C. conducive   D. effective   E. successive

14. Practically every municipality has fire ORDINANCES. ORDINANCES means *most nearly*   14.__

     A. drills   B. stations   C. engines   D. laws   E. problems

15. When the smoke cleared away, the firemen's task was ALLEVIATED. ALLEVIATED means *most nearly*   15.__

     A. lessened   B. visible   C. appreciated
     D. safer   E. accomplished

KEY (CORRECT ANSWERS)

1.	A		6.	B
2.	C		7.	D
3.	C		8.	B
4.	E		9.	E
5.	E		10.	E

11.	C
12.	E
13.	E
14.	D
15.	A

WORD MEANING
EXAMINATION SECTION
TEST 1

DIRECTIONS : For the following questions, select the word or group of words lettered A, B, C, D, or E that means MOST NEARLY the same as the word in capital letters. *PRINT THE LETTER OF THE CORRECT ANSWER IN THE SPACE AT THE RIGHT.*

1. The CONFLAGRATION spread throughout the entire city.   1.____

   A. hostilities   B. confusion   C. rumor   D. epidemic   E. fire

2. The firemen PURGED the gas tank after emptying its contents.   2.____

   A. sealed   B. punctured   C. exposed   D. cleansed   E. buried

3. Rules must be applied with DISCRETION.   3.____

   A. impartiality   B. judgment   C. severity
   D. patience   E. consistency

4. The officer and his men ASCENDED the stairs as rapidly as they could.   4.____

   A. went up   B. washed down   C. chopped
   D. shored up   E. inspected

5. The store's refusal to accept delivery of the merchandise was a violation of the   5.____
   EXPRESS provisions of the contract.

   A. clear   B. implied
   C. penalty   D. disputed
   E. complicated

6. Mr. Walsh could not attend the luncheon because he had a PRIOR appointment.   6.____

   A. conflicting   B. official   C. previous
   D. important   E. subsequent

7. The time allowed to complete the task was not ADEQUATE.   7.____

   A. long   B. enough   C. excessive   D. required   E. stated

8. The investigation unit began an EXTENSIVE search for the information.   8.____

   A. complicated   B. superficial   C. thorough
   D. leisurely   E. cursory

9. The secretary answered the telephone in a COURTEOUS manner.   9.____

   A. businesslike   B. friendly
   C. formal   D. gruff
   E. polite

10. The RECIPIENT of the money checked the total amount.   10.

     A. receiver   B. carrier   C. borrower   D. giver   E. sender

11. The College offered a variety of SEMINARS to upperclassmen.   11.

     A. reading courses with no formal supervision
     B. study courses for small groups of students engaged in research under a teacher
     C. guidance conferences with grade advisors
     D. work experience in different occupational fields
     E. luncheon discussions

12. The Dean pointed out that the FOCUS of the study was not clear.   12.

     A. end   B. objective   C. follow-up   D. location   E. basis

13. The faculty of the Anthropology Department agreed that the departmental program was DEFICIENT.   13.

     A. excellent   B. inadequate   C. demanding   D. sufficient   E. dilatory

14. The secretary was asked to type a rough draft of a course SYLLABUS.   14.

     A. directory of departments and services   B. examination schedule
     C. outline of a course of study   D. rules and regulations
     E. schedule of meetings

15. There is an item in a painting contract relating to INSOLVENCY.   15.

     A. the improper mixing of paint
     B. the use of improper materials
     C. taking excessive time to complete the contract
     D. bankruptcy
     E. the use of water

KEY (CORRECT ANSWERS)

1.	E	6.	C	11.	B
2.	D	7.	B	12.	B
3.	B	8.	C	13.	B
4.	A	9.	E	14.	C
5.	A	10.	A	15.	D

TEST 2

DIRECTIONS : For the following questions, select the word or group of words lettered A, B, C, D, or E that means MOST NEARLY the same as the word in capital letters. *PRINT THE LETTER OF THE CORRECT ANSWER IN THE SPACE AT THE RIGHT.*

1. The number of applicants exceeded the ANTICIPATED figure.　　　　1.＿＿＿

   A. expected　　B. required　　C. revised　　D. necessary　　E. hoped-for

2. The clerk was told to COLLATE the pages of the report.　　　　2.＿＿＿

   A. destroy　　B. edit　　C. correct　　D. assemble　　E. fasten

3. Mr. Jones is not AUTHORIZED to release the information.　　　　3.＿＿＿

   A. inclined　　B. pleased　　C. permitted　　D. trained　　E. expected

4. The secretary chose an APPROPRIATE office for the meeting.　　　　4.＿＿＿

   A. empty　　　　　　　　　B. decorated
   C. nearby　　　　　　　　 D. suitable
   E. inexpensive

5. The employee performs a COMPLEX set of tasks each day.　　　　5.＿＿＿

   A. difficult　　B. important　　C. pleasant　　D. large　　E. secret

6. The foreman INVESTIGATED the sewer to see whether it was clogged.　　　6.＿＿＿

   A. compelled　　B. diverted　　C. opened　　D. improved　　E. examined

7. The foreman SUPERVISED the work closely.　　　　7.＿＿＿

   A. criticized　　　　　　　B. neglected
   C. praised　　　　　　　　D. superintended
   E. reviewed

8. ILLICIT connections are often found during sewer inspections.　　　　8.＿＿＿

   A. damaged　　B. legal　　C. poor　　D. unlawful　　E. clogged

9. The sewage in the manhole was floating SLUGGISHLY.　　　　9.＿＿＿

   A. buoyantly　　B. odiferously　　C. slowly　　D. swiftly　　E. evenly

10. It is most COMMON to find sewer pipes made of either clay or concrete.　　　10.＿＿＿

    A. characteristic　　　　B. inordinate　　　　C. prevalent
    D. retiring　　　　　　　E. vulgar

11. He needed public assistance because he was INCAPACITATED.　　　　11.＿＿＿

    A. uneducated　　　　　B. unreliable　　　　C. uncooperative
    D. discharged　　　　　E. disabled

12. The caseworker explained to the client that signing the document was COMPULSORY. 12.

    A. temporary   B. required
    C. different   D. comprehensive
    E. usual

13. The woman's actions did not JEOPARDIZE her eligibility for benefits. 13.

    A. delay   B. reinforce   C. determine   D. endanger   E. enhance

14. The material is PUTRESCIBLE. 14.

    A. compacted   B. liable to burn   C. heavy
    D. liable to rot   E. liable to clog

15. Older incinerator plants are handstoked and fed INTERMITTENTLY. 15.

    A. constantly   B. heavily   C. periodically
    D. with a shovel   E. every few minutes

KEY (CORRECT ANSWERS)

1.	A	6.	E	11.	E
2.	D	7.	D	12.	B
3.	C	8.	D	13.	D
4.	D	9.	C	14.	D
5.	A	10.	C	15.	C

TEST 3

DIRECTIONS : For the following questions, select the word or group of words lettered A, B, C, D, or E that means MOST NEARLY the same as the word in capital letters. *PRINT THE LETTER OF THE CORRECT ANSWER IN THE SPACE AT THE RIGHT.*

1. The foreman made an ABSURD remark.   1._____

   A. misleading   B. ridiculous   C. unfair   D. wicked   E. artful

2. The electrician was ADEPT at his job.   2._____

   A. co-operative   B. developed
   C. diligent   D. skilled
   E. inept

3. The foreman stated that the condition was GENERAL.   3._____

   A. artificial   B. prevalent   C. timely   D. transient   E. likely

4. The asphalt worker engages in a HAZARDOUS job.   4._____

   A. absorbing   B. dangerous   C. demanding
   D. difficult   E. uninteresting

5. The foreman made a TRIVIAL mistake.   5._____

   A. accidental   B. dangerous
   C. obvious   D. serious
   E. unimportant

6. No DEVIATION from the specifications will be allowed unless the same has been previ-   6._____
   ously authorized by the engineer.

   A. violation   B. variation   C. complete change
   D. authorized change   E. inference

7. The contractor shall SAFEGUARD all points, stakes, grade marks, monuments, and   7._____
   bench marks, made or established on or near the line of the work.

   A. watch closely   B. guard against theft
   C. prevent damage to   D. replace
   E. control

8. Bitumen-sand bed shall consist of sand with cut-back asphalt COMBINED in definite pro- 8._____
   portions by weight.

   A. together   B. mixed   C. added   D. placed   E. undiluted

9. The material was quite DESICCATED.   9._____

   A. hard   B. dangerous C. soft   D. spongy   E. dry

10. Malice was PATENT in all of his remarks.   10._____

    A. elevated   B. evident   C. threatening D. foreign   E. implicit

11. A Chaplain shall have the COMPARABLE rank of Inspector.   11.

   A. false   B. superior   C. equal   D. presumed E. ordinary

12. Pushcarts and DERELICT automobiles shall be delivered to the bureau of incum-   12.
    brances.

   A. dilapidated   B. abandoned   C. delinquent
   D. contraband   E. unusable

13. When the EXIGENCIES of the service shall so require, a captain may assign a patrol-   13.
    man from the outgoing platoon to house duty.

   A. needs   B. conveniences
   C. changes   D. increases
   E. exits

14. There is a provision for the award of a medal for merit for an act of outstanding bravery,   14.
    performed in the line of duty, at IMMINENT personal hazard of life.

   A. impending B. inherent   C. certain   D. great   E. eminent

15. A member of the department shall not communicate with a railroad company for the pur-   15.
    pose of EXPEDITING the issue of a transportation pass,

   A. extorting   B. procuring   C. demanding
   D. hastening   E. extending

KEY (CORRECT ANSWERS)

1.	B	6.	B	11.	C
2.	D	7.	C	12.	B
3.	B	8.	B	13.	A
4.	B	9.	E	14.	A
5.	E	10.	B	15.	D

TEST 4

DIRECTIONS : For the following questions, select the word or group of words lettered A, B, C, D, or E that means MOST NEARLY the same as the word in capital letters. *PRINT THE LETTER OF THE CORRECT ANSWER IN THE SPACE AT THE RIGHT.*

1. The EXTANT copies of the document were found in the safe.   1.____

   A. existing   B. original   C. forged   D. duplicate   E. torn

2. The recruit was more COMPLAISANT after the captain spoke to him.   2.____

   A. calm   B. affable   C. irritable   D. confident   E. arrogant

3. The man was captured under highly CREDITABLE circumstances.   3.____

   A. doubtful   B. believable   C. praiseworthy
   D. unexpected   E. unbelievable

4. The new employee appeared DIFFIDENT.   4.____

   A. contrary   B. haughty   C. conceited   D. unsure   E. confident

5. His superior officers were more SAGACIOUS than he.   5.____

   A. upset   B. obtuse   C. absurd   D. verbose   E. shrewd

_____

KEY (CORRECT ANSWERS)

1. A
2. B
3. C
4. D
5. E

_____

TESTS IN SENTENCE COMPLETION / 1 BLANK
EXAMINATION SECTION
TEST 1

DIRECTIONS: Each question in this section consists of a sentence in which one word is missing; a blank line indicates where the word has been removed from the sentence. Beneath each sentence are five words, *one* of which is the missing word. You are to select the letter of the missing word by deciding which one of the five words BEST fits in with the meaning of the sentence. *PRINT THE LETTER OF THE CORRECT ANSWER IN THE SPACE AT THE RIGHT.*

1. A man who cannot win honor in his own _____ will have a very small chance of winning it from posterity.

   A. right　　B. field　　C. country　　D. way　　E. age

1.____

2. The latent period for the contractile response to direct stimulation of the muscle has quite another and shorte value, encompassing only a utilization period. Hence it is that the term *latent period* must be _____ carefully each time that it is used.

   A. checked　　　　B. timed　　　　C. introduced
   D. defined　　　　E. selected

2.____

3. Many television watchers enjoy stories which contain violence. Consequently those television producers who are dominated by rating systems aim to _____ the popular taste.

   A. raise　　B. control　　C. gratify　　D. ignore　　E. lower

3.____

4. No other man loses so much, so _____, so absolutely, as the beaten candidate for high public office.

   A. bewilderingly　　　　B. predictably　　　　C. disgracefully
   D. publicly　　　　　　E. cheerfully

4.____

5. Mathematics is the product of thought operating by means of _____ for the purpose of expressing general laws.

   A. reasoning　　　　B. symbols　　　　C. words
   D. examples　　　　E. science

5.____

6. Deductive reasoning is that form of reasoning in which the conclusion must necessarily follow if we accept the premise as true. In deduction, it is _____ the premise to be true and the conclusion false.

   A. impossible　　　　B. inevitable　　　　C. reasonable
   D. surprising　　　　E. unlikely

6.____

7. Because in the administration it hath respect not to the group but to the _____, our form of government is called a democracy.

   A. courts　　　　B. people　　　　C. majority
   D. individual　　E. law

7.____

8. Before criticizing the work of an artist one needs to _____ the artist's purpose.   8.__

   A. understand   B. reveal   C. defend
   D. correct   E. change

9. Their work was commemorative in character and consisted largely of _____ erected   9.__
   upon the occasion of victories.

   A. towers   B. tombs   C. monuments
   D. castles   E. fortresses

10. Every good story is carefully contrived: the elements of the story are _____ to fit with   10.__
    one another in order to
    make an effect on the reader.

   A. read   B. learned   C. emphasized
   D. reduced   E. planned

———

KEY (CORRECT ANSWERS)

1. E	6. A
2. D	7. D
3. C	8. A
4. D	9. C
5. B	10. E

———

TEST 2

DIRECTIONS: Each question in this section consists of a sentence in which one word is missing; a blank line indicates where the word has been removed from the sentence. Beneath each sentence are five words, *one* of which is the missing word. You are to select the letter of the missing word by deciding which one of the five words BEST fits in with the meaning of the sentence. *PRINT THE LETTER OF THE CORRECT ANSWER IN THE SPACE AT THE RIGHT.*

1. One of the most prevalent erroneous contentions is that Argentina is a country of _____ agricultural resources and needs only the arrival of ambitious settlers.

    A. modernized   B. flourishing   C. undeveloped
    D. waning   E. limited

    1._____

2. The last official statistics for the town indicated the presence of 24,212 Italians, 6,450 Magyars, and 2,315 Germans, which ensures to the _____ a numerical preponderance.

    A. Germans   B. figures   C. town   D. Magyars   E. Italians

    2._____

3. Precision of wording is necessary in good writing; by choosing words that exactly convey the desired meaning, one can avoid _____.

    A. duplicity   B. incongruity   C. complexity
    D. ambiguity   E. implications

    3._____

4. Various civilians of the liberal school in the British Parliament remonstrated that there were no grounds for _____ of French aggression, since the Emperor showed less disposition to augment the navy than had Louis Philippe.

    A. suppression   B. retaliation   C. apprehension
    D. concealment   E. commencement

    4._____

5. _____ is as clear and definite as any of our urges; we wonder what is in a sealed letter or what is being said in a telephone booth.

    A. Envy   B. Curiosity   C. Knowledge
    D. Communication   E. Ambition

    5._____

6. It is a rarely philosophic soul who can make a _____ the other alternative forever into the limbo of forgotten things.

    A. mistake   B. wish   C. change   D. choice   E. plan

    6._____

7. A creditor is worse than a master. A master owns only your person, but a creditor owns your _____ as well.

    A. aspirations   B. potentialities   C. ideas
    D. dignity   E. wealth

    7._____

8. People _____ small faults, in order to insinuate that they have no great ones.

    A. create   B. display   C. confess   D. seek   E. reject

    8._____

9. Andrew Jackson believed that wars were inevitable, and to him the length and irregularity of our coast presented a _____ that called for a more than merely passive navy.

    A. defense   B. barrier   C. provocation
    D. vulnerability   E. dispute

9.___

10. The progressive yearly _____ of the land, caused by the depositing of mud from the river, makes it possible to estimate the age of excavated remains by noting the depth at which they are found below the present level of the valley.

    A. erosion   B. elevation   C. improvement
    D. irrigation   E. displacement

10.___

KEY (CORRECT ANSWERS)

1.	C	6.	D
2.	E	7.	D
3.	D	8.	C
4.	C	9.	D
5.	B	10.	B

TEST 3

DIRECTIONS: Each question in this section consists of a sentence in which one word is missing; a blank line indicates where the word has been removed from the sentence. Beneath each sentence are five words, *one* of which is the missing word. You are to select the letter of the missing word by deciding which one of the five words BEST fits in with the meaning of the sentence. *PRINT THE LETTER OF THE CORRECT ANSWER IN THE SPACE AT THE RIGHT.*

1. The judge exercised commendable _____ dismissing the charge against the prisoner. In spite of the clamor that surrounded the trial, and the heinousness of the offense, the judge could not be swayed to overlook the lack of facts in the case.   1.____

   A.   avidity   B.   meticulousness   C.   clemency
   D.   balance   E.   querulousness

2. The pianist played the concerto _____, displaying such facility and skill as has rarely been matched in this old auditorium.   2.____

   A.   strenuous   B.   spiritedly   C.   passionately
   D.   casually   E.   deftly

3. The Tanglewood Symphony Orchestra holds its outdoor concerts far from city turmoil in a _____, bucolic setting.   3.____

   A.   spectacular   B.   atavistic   C.   serene
   D.   chaotic   E.   catholic

4. Honest satire gives true joy to the thinking man. Thus, the satirist is most _____ when he points out the hypocrisy in human actions.   4.____

   A.   elated   B.   humiliated   C.   ungainly
   D.   repressed   E.   disdainful

5. She was a(n) _____ preferred the company of her books to the pleasures of cafe society.   5.____

   A.   philanthropist   B.   stoic   C.   exhibitionist
   D.   extrovert   E.   introvert

6. So many people are so convinced that people are driven by _____ motives that they cannot believe that anybody is unselfish!   6.____

   A.   interior   B.   ulterior   C.   unworth
   D.   selfish   E.   destructive

7. These _____ results were brought about by a chain of fortuitous events.   7.____

   A.   unfortunate   B.   odd   C.   harmful
   D.   haphazard   E.   propitious

8. The bank teller's _____ of the funds was discovered the following month when the auditors examined the books.   8.____

   A.   embezzlement   B.   burglary   C.   borrowing
   D.   assignment   E.   theft

9. The monks gathered in the _____ for their evening meal. 9.__

    A. lounge   B. auditorium   C. refectory
    D. rectory   E. solarium

10. Local officials usually have the responsibility in each area of determining when the need   10.__
is sufficiently great to _____ withdrawals from the community water supply.

    A. encourage   B. justify   C. discontinue
    D. advocate   E. forbid

———

KEY (CORRECT ANSWERS)

1.	D	6.	B
2.	E	7.	D
3.	C	8.	A
4.	A	9.	C
5.	E	10.	B

———

TEST 4

DIRECTIONS: Each question in this section consists of a sentence in which one word is missing; a blank line indicates where the word has been removed from the sentence. Beneath each sentence are five words, *one* of which is the missing word. You are to select the letter of the missing word by deciding which one of the five words BEST fits in with the meaning of the sentence. *PRINT THE LETTER OF THE CORRECT ANSWER IN THE SPACE AT THE RIGHT*

1. The life of the mining camps as portrayed by Bret Harte—boisterous, material, brawling— was in direct _____ to the contemporary Eastern world of conventional morals and staid deportment depicted by other men of letters.

   A. model   B. parallel   C. antithesis
   D. relationship   E. response

   1._____

2. The agreements were to remain in force for three years and were subject to automatic _____ unless terminated by the parties concerned on one month's notice.

   A. renewal   B. abrogation   C. amendment
   D. confiscation   E. option

   2._____

3. In a democracy, people are recognized for what they do rather than for their _____.

   A. alacrity   B. ability   C. reputation
   D. skill   E. pedigree

   3._____

4. Although he had often loudly proclaimed his _____ concerning world affairs, he actually read widely and was usually the best informed person in his circle.

   A. weariness   B. complacency   C. condolence
   D. indifference   E. worry

   4._____

5. This student holds the _____ record of being the sole failure in his class.

   A. flagrant   B. unhappy   C. egregious
   D. dubious   E. unusual

   5._____

6. She became enamored _____ acrobat when she witnessed his act.

   A. of   B. with   C. for   D. by   E. about

   6._____

7. This will _____ all previous wills.

   A. abrogates   B. denies   C. supersedes
   D. prevents   E. continues

   7._____

8. In the recent terrible Chicago _____, over ninety children were found dead as a result of the fire.

   A. hurricane   B. destruction   C. panic
   D. holocaust   E. accident

   8._____

9. I can ascribe no better reason why he shunned society than that he was a _____.

   A. mentor   B. Centaur   C. aristocrat
   D. misanthrope   E. failure

   9._____

10. One who attempts to learn all the known facts before he comes to a conclusion may most   10.___
    aptly be described as a _____.

    A. realist   B. philosopher   C. cynic
    D. pessimist   E. skeptic

———————

KEY (CORRECT ANSWERS)

1.	C		6.	A
2.	A		7.	C
3.	E		8.	D
4.	D		9.	D
5.	D		10.	E

———————

TEST 5

DIRECTIONS: Each question in this section consists of a sentence in which one word is missing; a blank line indicates where the word has been removed from the sentence. Beneath each sentence are five words, *one* of which is the missing word. You are to select the letter of the missing word by deciding which one of the five words BEST fits in with the meaning of the sentence. *PRINT THE LETTER OF THE CORRECT ANSWER IN THE SPACE AT THE RIGHT.*

1. The prime minister, fleeing from the rebels who had seized the government, sought _____ in the church.   1.____

   A. revenge   B. mercy   C. relief
   D. salvation   E. sanctuary

2. It does not take us long to conclude that it is foolish to fight the _____, and that it is far wiser to accept it.   2.____

   A. inevitable   B. inconsequential   C. impossible
   D. choice   E. invasion

3. _____ is usually defined as an excessively high rate of interest.   3.____

   A. Injustice   B. Perjury   C. Exorbitant
   D. Embezzlement   E. Usury

4. "I ask you, gentlemen of the jury, to find this man guilty since I have _____ the charges brought about him."   4.____

   A. documented   B. questioned   C. revised
   D. selected   E. confused

5. Although the critic was a close friend of the producer, he told him that he could not _____ his play.   5.____

   A. condemn   B. prefer   C. congratulate
   D. endorse   E. revile

6. Knowledge of human nature and motivation is an important _____ in all areas of endeavor.   6.____

   A. object   B. incentive   C. opportunity
   D. asset   E. goal

7. Numbered among the audience were kings, princes, dukes, and even a maharajah, all attempting to _____ another in the glitter of their habiliments and the number of their escorts.   7.____

   A. supersede   B. outdo   C. guide
   D. vanquish   E. equal

8. There seems to be a widespread feeling that peoples who are located below us in respect to latitude are _____ also in respect to intellect and ability.   8.____

   A. superior   B. melodramatic   C. inferior
   D. ulterior   E. contemptible

9. This should be considered a(n) _____ rather than the usual occurrence.   9.__

    A. coincidence   B. specialty   C. development
    D. outgrowth   E. mirage

10. Those who were considered states' rights adherents in the early part of our history,   10.__
espoused the diminution of the powers of the national government because they had
always been _____ of these powers.

    A. solicitous   B. advocates   C. apprehensive
    D. mindful   E. respectful

KEY (CORRECT ANSWERS)

1.	E	6.	D
2.	A	7.	B
3.	E	8.	C
4.	A	9.	A
5.	D	10.	C

TEST 6

DIRECTIONS: Each question in this section consists of a sentence in which one word is missing; a blank line indicates where the word has been removed from the sentence. Beneath each sentence are five words, *one* of which is the missing word. You are to select the letter of the missing word by deciding which one of the five words BEST fits in with the meaning of the sentence. *PRINT THE LETTER OF THE CORRECT ANSWER IN THE SPACE AT THE RIGHT.*

1. We can see in retrospect that the high hopes for lasting peace conceived at Versailles in 1919 were _____.   1.____

   A. ingenuous   B. transient   C. nostalgic
   D. ingenious   E. specious

2. One of the constructive effects of Nazism was the passage by the U.N. of a resolution to combat _____.   2.____

   A. armaments   B. nationalism   C. colonialism
   D. genocide   E. geriatrics

3. In our prisons, the role of _____ often gains for certain inmates a powerful position among their fellow prisoners.   3.____

   A. informer   B. clerk   C. warden   D. trusty   E. turnkey

4. It is the _____ liar, experienced in the ways of the world, who finally trips upon some incongruous detail.   4.____

   A. consummate   B. incorrigible   C. congenital
   D. lagrant   E. contemptible

5. Anyone who is called a misogynist can hardly be expected to look upon women with _____ contemptuous eyes.   5.____

   A. more than   B. nothing less than   C. decidedly
   D. other than   E. always

6. Demagogues such as Hitler and Mussolini aroused the masses by appealing to their _____ rather than to their intellect.   6.____

   A. emotions   B. reason   C. nationalism
   D. conquests   E. duty

7. He was in great demand as an entertainer for his _____ abilities: he could sing, dance, tell a joke, or relate a story with equally great skill and facility.   7.____

   A. versatile   B. logical   C. culinary
   D. histrionic   E. creative

8. The wise politician is aware that, next to knowing when to seize an opportunity, it is also important to know when to _____ an advantage.   8.____

   A. develop   B. seek   C. revise
   D. proclaim   E. forego

9. Books on psychology inform us that the best way to break a bad habit is to _____ a new habit in its place.   9.__

    A. expel   B. substitute   C. conceal
    D. curtail   E. supplant

10. The author who uses one word where another uses a whole paragraph, should be considered a _____ writer.   10.__

    A. successful   B. grandiloquent   C. experienced
    D. prolix   E. succinct

KEY (CORRECT ANSWERS)

1.	A	6.	A
2.	D	7.	A
3.	A	8.	E
4.	A	9.	B
5.	D	10.	E

CPSIA information can be obtained
at www.ICGtesting.com
Printed in the USA
LVHW050146020323
740759LV00013B/533